# Cambridge Elements

Elements in Global Philosophy of Religion
edited by
Yujin Nagasawa
*University of Oklahoma*

# AFRO-BRAZILIAN
# RELIGIONS

José Eduardo Porcher
*Pontifical Catholic University of Rio de Janeiro*

CAMBRIDGE
UNIVERSITY PRESS

# CAMBRIDGE
## UNIVERSITY PRESS

Shaftesbury Road, Cambridge CB2 8EA, United Kingdom

One Liberty Plaza, 20th Floor, New York, NY 10006, USA

477 Williamstown Road, Port Melbourne, VIC 3207, Australia

314–321, 3rd Floor, Plot 3, Splendor Forum, Jasola District Centre, New Delhi – 110025, India

103 Penang Road, #05–06/07, Visioncrest Commercial, Singapore 238467

Cambridge University Press is part of Cambridge University Press & Assessment, a department of the University of Cambridge.

We share the University's mission to contribute to society through the pursuit of education, learning and research at the highest international levels of excellence.

www.cambridge.org
Information on this title: www.cambridge.org/9781009469036

DOI: 10.1017/9781009469029

© José Eduardo Porcher 2024

When citing this work, please include a reference to the DOI 10.1017/9781009469029

First published 2024

A catalogue record for this publication is available from the British Library.

ISBN 978-1-009-46903-6 Hardback
ISBN 978-1-009-46901-2 Paperback
ISSN 2976-5749 (online)
ISSN 2976-5730 (print)

# Afro-Brazilian Religions

Elements in Global Philosophy of Religion

DOI: 10.1017/9781009469029
First published online: November 2024

José Eduardo Porcher
*Pontifical Catholic University of Rio de Janeiro*

**Author for correspondence**: José Eduardo Porcher, jeporcher@gmail.com

**Abstract:** This Element introduces Afro-Brazilian religions and underscores the necessity for an expanded methodological framework to encompass these traditions in the philosophy of religion. It emphasizes the importance of incorporating overlooked sources like mythic narratives and ethnographies while acknowledging the pivotal role of material culture in cognitive processes. Furthermore, it advocates for adopting an embodiment paradigm to facilitate the development of a philosophy of religious practice. The Element illustrates this approach by examining phenomena often neglected in philosophical discussions on religion, such as sacrifice and spirit possession, and delves into the ontological commitments and implications of these practices. It also stresses the significance of employing thick descriptions and embracing interdisciplinary dialogue to cultivate a globally inclusive philosophy of religion, capable of engaging with phenomena frequently sidelined within the mainstream.

**Keywords:** Afro-Brazilian religions, philosophy of religious practice, sacrifice, spirit possession, embodied knowledge

ISBNs: 9781009469036 (HB), 9781009469012 (PB), 9781009469029 (OC)
ISSNs: 2976-5749 (online), 2976-5730 (print)

# Contents

## Opening

I'll teach you differences.
Shakespeare, *King Lear*, Act 1, Scene 4

Responding to Richard Rorty's verdict that "Western liberal intellectuals should accept the fact that we have to start from where we are, and that this means that there are lots of visions which we simply cannot take seriously" (1991, 29), Eduardo Viveiros de Castro confronts the prevalent ethnocentric bias within Western philosophy and defines his own discipline, anthropology, in reactive and starkly contrasting terms: "taking seriously what Western intellectuals cannot, so Rorty tells us, take seriously" (2011, 133). In this Element, I propose to follow through Viveiros de Castro's directive and apply it to the philosophy of religion by exploring mythic narratives, presenting the practices of sacrifice, initiation, and spirit possession as they occur in Afro-Brazilian traditions, and by considering some of the methodological expansions required for the philosophy of religion to genuinely acknowledge and engage with these practices and traditions, which have thus far been overlooked.

In the last fifteen years or so, the philosophy of religion has withstood mounting attacks on its methodology, scope, and motivations, but it has been slow to change. Many see it as a discipline in which, on the one hand, outside influences, such as upbringing and education, play a pernicious role, and on the other, a tendency to explore and even formulate its questions solely in terms of its own practitioners' traditions is prevalent (De Cruz, 2018). The titles of recent monographs and edited volumes have announced its end, questioned its purpose, called for its renewal and reconfiguration, and wondered what its future might look like. To date, perhaps no work has more forcefully argued for overhauling the philosophy of religion than Kevin Schilbrack's *Philosophy and the Study of Religions: A Manifesto* (Schilbrack, 2014).

Schilbrack diagnoses traditional philosophy of religion as narrow, intellectualist, and insular. Narrowness refers to the fact that it suffers from a very restricted diet of examples. Even though attention to traditions other than Christianity has been growing, the two main branches of the discipline – natural theology and epistemology of religion – engage disproportionately with Christian theology. Intellectualism refers to the fact that the philosophy of religion is biased toward the analysis and assessment of religious beliefs to the exclusion of other practical religious phenomena, such as rituals, pilgrimages, feasts, and dietary laws. Finally, insularity refers to the lack of connection between the philosophy of religion and other disciplines in the academic study of religion and even from different fields within philosophy. Traditional philosophy of religion, Schilbrack remarks, does not "play well with others" (2014, 20).

In ignoring so many traditions, the questions philosophers of religion ask (and the answers they offer) reveal a degree of religious illiteracy that throws doubt on its relevance to the academic study of religion and on whether it even deserves the name philosophy of *religion*. The discipline must thus expand its current focus to become a global form of critical reflection on religions in all their varieties and dimensions in dialogue with other branches of philosophy and with other disciplines of the academic study of religions. As Timothy Knepper maintains, if one wants to philosophize about religion, then "one needs to understand religion in all its messy cultural-historical diversity. Insofar as one considers only a limited set of traditions or reasons, one's philosophy of religion is limited" (2013, 76). Yet, as soon as we try to bring new religious traditions into the fold of the philosophy of religion, especially ones that are ritual-focused and orally transmitted, we are faced with the question of how to go about this task. The discipline has paid almost no attention to ritual, even the ritual life of those religions that have received pride of place within it. Philosophers will not be able to rely on the same sources when thinking about religions that are not codified, text-based, institutionally centralized, and do not have a theological tradition as input (Porcher, 2024).

While Afro-Brazilian traditions are not text-based and have not developed systematic theologies, cultural anthropologists and ethnographers have attended to them for nearly a century. To contemplate these traditions, then, it is thus not a matter of choice but of necessity to do philosophy of religion that engages with narrative and ethnographic sources and that pays attention to the non-doctrinal dimensions of religion. Taking this direction means expanding and re-evaluating the discipline's methodology and raising questions that can be an antidote to narrowness, intellectualism, and insularity. For instance: what does it mean to consider the religious person as an embodied subject? How should the material, affective, and social aspects of religious rituals figure in an explanation of religious cognition? How can we engage philosophically with religious practices without sanitizing or homogenizing them? In this Element, I will explore these questions to begin doing conceptual justice to Afro-Brazilian religions[1] while sketching a methodology for a philosophy of religious practice.

In Section 1, I begin to present Afro-Brazilian religions, their social and historical context, and their prototypical features, almost all of which have fallen outside the scope of traditional philosophy of religion. In Section 2,

---

[1] The term is synonymous with "African-derived religions in Brazil" (and the Portuguese "religiões brasileiras de matriz africana"). I choose "Afro-Brazilian religions" for brevity, while acknowledging that it encompasses a spectrum of traditions. Some of these are more directly derived from African traditions, while others are less so, but all explicitly incorporate African elements.

I draw on the oral literature of Candomblé and on extant discussions within African philosophical scholarship to offer a first look at the theology borne by its mythic narratives. In Section 3, I turn to ethnography to locate the meaning of the fundamental practice of blood sacrifice and to begin homing in on the emic concept of *axé*, the spiritual life force believed to permeate everything and everyone. In Section 4, I delve into material culture as it relates to initiation, drawing on cognitive ethnography and cultural anthropology to support an interpretation of Candomblé's view of ontology, personhood, and agency. Finally, in Section 5, I focus on the embodied, situated, and materially extended practices of dance and spirit possession to defend the adoption of a theoretical framework in the philosophy of religion that recognizes such practices as forms of embodied knowledge.

## 1 Afro-Brazilian Religions

Between 1500 and the 1860s, upward of four million enslaved Africans were forcefully taken to Brazil, a remarkable figure that accounted for nearly 40 percent of all individuals made to endure the transatlantic journey, surpassing the number sent to the United States by more than tenfold (Bergad, 2007).[2] These individuals, hailing from diverse African ethnic backgrounds, became intertwined, notably in Brazil's early capitals, Salvador and Rio de Janeiro. They brought their languages, deities, rituals, cuisine, dances, and music, which blended with traditions from other enslaved groups and with the Roman Catholicism introduced by Portuguese colonizers. This intricate amalgamation gave rise to variegated families of traditions such as Candomblé in the state of Bahia, Xangô in Pernambuco, Tambor de Mina in Maranhão, Batuque in Rio Grande do Sul, and others.

In Brazil, the diasporic worship traditions of enslaved Africans underwent significant transformations due to the profound disruption of their previous social, political, and religious structures by the exigencies of slavery. Forced to adapt to an entirely different societal context as laborers and confronted with the eradication of their former organizational frameworks, they also had to navigate the practice of their religion within a hostile environment while preserving their cultural customs within the constraints of oppressive slave culture. Nonetheless, the persecution persisted even following the abolition of slavery in 1888, intensifying during the Third Brazilian Republic from 1937 to 1945. Legal safeguards for religious freedom in Brazil were not established

---

[2] SlaveVoyages.org, a database hosted at Rice University, gathered data on 34,948 transatlantic slave voyages from 1501 to 1867 and estimates the number of enslaved Africans brought to Brazil at 5,848,266.

until 1946 but, regrettably, even after the enactment of these laws, challenges to Afro-Brazilian religions persist to this day. Consequently, Afro-Brazilian religions stand as a testament to a history of resistance and the evolution of Black and Afro-descendant identities, as diverse African ethnic groups reshaped their practices in the diaspora to sustain daily life under oppressive conditions (Engler and Brito, 2016).

These traditions possess no central authority with the power to determine doctrine and orthodoxy. Each temple (*terreiro*) or community of practitioners is ultimately autonomous, approaching the religion in ways informed by their tradition and leadership. Yet, in some cases, there are clearly delineating boundaries between lineages, each more or less closely linked to specific African ethnic traditions. Thus, the landscape of Afro-diasporic religions in Brazil is richly varied, and includes traditions such as Babassuê, Batuque, Jarê, Omolocô, Pajelança de Negro, Quimbanda, Tambor de Mina, Terecô, Umbanda, Xambá, Xangô, and others. Pride of place, however, is usually given to Candomblé for historical, cultural, and demographic, if not simply chronological, reasons. Candomblé is a family of religious traditions, subdivided into "nations," that developed in Brazil mainly during the nineteenth century. It will be the main focus of this Element, even though I will also discuss traditions such as Xangô and Batuque (in Sections 4 and 5) which developed in parallel to Candomblé and to which the morals I will draw in the course of this investigation also apply.

Two main ethnic groups were predominantly brought to Brazil during the transatlantic slave trade (Carneiro, 1948/2019). The first group, often referred to as the Western "Sudanese," included the Yoruba (known as Nagô in Brazil), the Ewe and Fon peoples (referred to as Jêje), and the Ashanti. They originated from present-day West African nations like Nigeria, Ghana, Benin, and Togo, and primarily arrived through the port of Salvador and worked in northeastern sugar mills between the seventeenth and nineteenth centuries. The second group, pertaining to the Bantu ethnolinguistic grouping, consisted mostly of the Angolans, Kasanje, and Mbangala from present-day Congo, Angola, and Mozambique. They primarily arrived through the port of Rio de Janeiro and worked along the Brazilian coast and in interior regions, particularly between the present-day states of Minas Gerais and Goiás. Each lineage or nation seeks to maintain its own deities, rituals, songs, drumming rhythms, and ceremonial customs, with practitioners primarily affiliating with one of these nations. Nevertheless, there has been significant intermingling between nations, to the point that many *terreiros* identify as Jêje-Nagô, for instance (Lima, 1977).

Candomblé ritual worship centers on the invocation and celebration of African deities most commonly referred to as *orixás* (from the Yoruba *òrìṣà*,[3] as well as semi-divine ancestors (*eguns*), and powerful spirits.[4] These constitute a pantheon of deities who were either created by or emerged from the Supreme Being, Olorum (also known as Olodumare).[5] As we will see in Section 2, although there are no specific myths, shrines, or ritual practices centered around the high god of Candomblé, the Supreme Being nevertheless plays a significant role in myths related to the origins of existence and the creation of the earthly realm. In that pre-creation state, only the spiritual realm existed. Following Yoruba mythology, Candomblé envisions the spiritual realm as comprising two distinct spheres: a higher and a lower one. The higher sphere is where the Supreme Being resides. The second heavenly sphere exists in close proximity to the earthly realm and serves as the abode for the *orixás* as well as the ancestors (Elbein dos Santos, 1976/2012).

Candomblé teaches that every human being is governed by specific *orixás*. Most *orixás* are associated with specific elements of nature believed to possess and impart the energy of that specific deity. In Candomblé worship, key female deities include Oxum (associated with freshwater), Iemanjá (related to the sea, see Figure 1), Iansã (also known as Oiá, connected with the wind), and Nanã (associated with mud). Among the main male deities are Ogum (the deity of war and iron), Xangô (linked with quarries and thunder), Oxóssi (related to hunting and forests), and Obaluaiê (also known as Omulu, associated with healing and infectious diseases). Moreover, each of these deities has been syncretized with particular Catholic saints who have been the object of popular devotion in Brazil since colonial times. The prevailing narrative among practitioners asserts that the Afro-Catholic syncretism in Afro-Brazilian religions was a response to the prohibition against enslaved Africans worshipping their own deities. For instance, Oxóssi, often depicted with a bow and arrow, was syncretized with Saint George in Bahia and Saint Sebastian in Rio de Janeiro. Such syncretism is thus commonly likened to a mask, as enslaved Africans would have incorporated Catholic saints into their religious practices to disguise their worship of African deities, thereby safeguarding their traditions. As Ayodeji Ogunnaike (2020) notes, recent decades have witnessed a movement among Candomblé practitioners to "re-Africanize" their traditions by symbolically removing the

---

[3] All subsequent parenthetical additions to Brazilian Portuguese words in the vocabulary of Candomblé will refer to the Yoruba words from which they originate.

[4] The deities are also referred to as *voduns* (from the Fon and Ewe languages) in Candomblé Jêje and *inquices* (from the Bantu *nkisi*) in Candomblé Angola – the two main nations of Candomblé along with Queto (Nagô). In this Element, I will employ the Yoruba-derived terminology of Candomblé Nagô. I choose this terminology because of its widespread usage and for brevity.

[5] This method of worship forms the basis of several religious traditions born in the context of New World slavery, such as the Cuban tradition of Lucumí (also known as Regla de Ocha or Santería) and the traditions of Haitian Vodou and Dominican Vudú.

**Figure 1** Feast of Iemanjá in Rio Grande do Sul (2017)
Photograph by Wagner Ludwig Malta. Used with permission.

white masks from their deities and, in many cases, effectively removing every last shred of Afro-Catholic syncretism from their practice.

Rita Amaral (2002) underscores the significance of celebration (*xirê*) in Candomblé, emphasizing its role in fostering community engagement, transmitting values, and shaping devotees' worldviews. These celebrations are integral to Candomblé's identity, symbolizing the connection between the divine and the human, with an emphasis on experiencing the sacred as a source of sensory delight. Furthermore, Yvonne Daniel (2005), in describing dancing in Candomblé, appeals to the concept of embodied knowledge as transformative, leading to a profound shift in perception and spiritual inspiration. As we will see in Section 5, embodied activities of dancing, singing, and drumming serve as a means of connecting with history, divinity, and ancestry through one's body.

Significantly, the *orixás* are believed to take literal attendance during ceremonies. Spirit possession (or incorporation) entails the temporary displacement of a person's conscious self by a more powerful, immaterial being during a state of trance (Seligman, 2014). Spirit possession mediums forge lasting connections with the entities, facilitating their periodic emergence in the earthly world. As a result, these mediums frequently undergo profound transformations in their self-awareness and physical autonomy. During trance states, their everyday self-awareness temporarily fades, and their bodies operate devoid of personal intent. It is common for the medium to later recount having no memory of the events during incorporation. Yet, they recognize that their actions have been guided by a consciousness distinct from their regular identity and intentions.

As we will see in Section 4, however, the entity that "comes down" during possession and engages with humans is not perceived as an abstract entity but as one of its myriad manifestations, existing solely within the tangible embodiment of a specific individual (Segato, 2005, 98). For instance, when someone is discussing the actions of the *orixá* who has descended in incorporation, they will never refer to them in general but will always specify the *orixá* of a particular person: "Julio's Xangô did/said ..." The personal nature of each person's *orixá* becomes apparent in how they are envisioned by their respective followers, where the *orixá* of each person possesses a distinctly unique visage and physical characteristics (Schmidt, 2016, 113). Furthermore, the degree of reverence shown to an incorporated *orixá* is closely linked to the hierarchical position held by the incorporating medium.

While generic *orixás* exist in a dimension beyond human space and time, a person's *orixá* is "born" when the medium is initiated, something which is reflected in the fact that initiation is called *feitura* (the process of being "made," *feito*). Marcio Goldman (2007) observes that an individual is not born ready-made but is rather constructed during the prolonged initiation process. More than that, the initial possession experience serves as the catalyst for shaping both the individual and the *orixá*. Goldman's assertion revolves around the idea that the generic *orixá* only gains individuality when it incorporates in a human being. The ultimate result of this initiation process is that "an individual, previously undifferentiated, transforms into a structured person, and a generic *orixá* is brought into existence as an individual *orixá*" (2007, p. 112).

The initiation process spans several days (or weeks), with the initiate sequestered within the temple, and includes ritual baths and cleansings (*ebós*) for purification and protection. Simultaneously, the initiate strengthens their head (*ori*) through a meal offering (*bori*), as we will see in Section 3. With the head fortified, the main initiation ceremony follows, involving head-shaving, ritual consecration, and often an animal sacrifice, with blood symbolically extended to the material representation of the deity, known as its seat (*assento*) or settlement (*assentamento*) – most often stones or metal tools, depending on the "saint," as we will see in Section 4. This seals a sacred alliance among the initiate, the *orixá*, its sacred symbols, and the overseeing priestess or priest.[6]

---

[6] For the sake of brevity, from now on I will shorten this to "priestess."

After the sacrificial act (*orô*), the initiate, now an *iaô*, exits seclusion and is publicly introduced in a celebration during which the *orixá* is fully adorned before engaging in their inaugural dance (see Figure 2). Initiation ceremonies strengthen group identity and emphasize the sacredness of the knowledge held within the community. This sense of exclusivity empowers individuals, granting them a unique and revered status.

Because of its initiatory character and the fact that its racialized identity was forged in resistance to institutional racism, secrecy in Candomblé serves a multifaceted role, encompassing several critical dimensions, acting as a criterion for membership, a measure of authority, and a determinant of ritual and initiational efficacy. Additionally, it plays a vital role in the construction of the power of sacred entities and serves as a means of advertisement and market positioning within the tradition. Initiates bear the responsibility of safeguarding sacred knowledge, ensuring its protection from dilution or misuse, thereby nurturing a strong sense of belonging and exclusivity among practitioners. However, as Paul Christopher Johnson (2002) observes, secrecy extends beyond

**Figure 2** Inaugural dance of Oxum in a terreiro in São Paulo (2010)
Photograph by Bettina Schmidt. Used with permission.

the mere withholding of information, encompassing bodily containment and the creation of a "closed body" (*corpo fechado*) through the initiation processes of making the head, seating the saint, and spatial reclusion – processes united around the shared tropes of open and closed, which are in turn related to safeguarding *axé* (*àṣẹ*), the spiritual life force which permeates all aspects of existence in Candomblé, from the inanimate to the living.

The equilibrium of *axé* is paramount to individual well-being, and neglecting ritual obligations to honor the *orixás* depletes one's *axé*, leading to all sorts of problems. But *axé* can be replenished through ceremonies, particularly initiation and sacrifice, rooted in the belief in a reciprocal relationship between humans and *orixás*. Honoring the *orixás* is thus a vital duty. As we will see in Section 3, blood sacrifices are central in Candomblé, and involve offering animals to the *orixás*, with blood believed to be the main vehicle of *axé* (Léo Neto *et al.*, 2009). While the *orixás* do not literally eat the sacrificial offerings, they absorb its *axé* (Schmidt, 2013). Estélio Gomberg's (2011) portrayal of sacrifice as a remedy highlights its sacred essence, emphasizing that every action bears deep significance, with no drop of blood shed in vain. This underscores the pivotal role of *axé*, as any imbalance can result in disruptions, spanning the realms of physical, mental, and social well-being.

Healing is thus a key aspect of Candomblé practice in two respects. First, Candomblé *terreiros* offer help for spiritual and physical issues. People initially seek these *terreiros* to understand the reasons behind their problems and suffering. To alleviate distress, various practices are used, including *ebó*, *bori*, herbal remedies, baths, blessings, potions, cleansing, and counseling. Offerings to the *orixás* are also made to request, undo, or express gratitude for specific outcomes. Second, and relatedly, healing is very commonly part of the narrative of one's initiation. As Rebecca Seligman (2014) notes, in spirit possession mediumship, the fusion of meaning and lived experience frequently leads to a profound self-transformation, which is a source of healing for many participants. This transformation involves a fundamental change in how individuals perceive and relate to themselves and others. As a result, this redefined sense of self plays a crucial role in the healing process, addressing not only social and emotional issues but also contributing to the relief of physical ailments.

Alongside *axé*, *odu* is a mainstay of the Candomblé worldview (Silva and Brumana, 2016). *Odu* represents an individual's life path and destiny. At birth, a child's *odu* is revealed, and aligning one's actions with this prescribed *odu* is crucial to avoid misfortune and attract good fortune. The influence of one's *odu* extends to all aspects of existence which are uncovered through divination sessions. Divining one's destiny in Candomblé typically employs 16 cowries (*búzios*), with their position, facing up or down, enabling diviners to consult the *orixás* on behalf of the community or for personal matters, "peeking behind the curtain of life," as it were (Flaksman, 2016, 18). Divination also offers guidance to clients seeking solutions, irrespective of their religious affiliation. The specific *odu* unveiled by the cowries is also instrumental in determining the identity of an individual's *orixá*. Both humans and *orixás* share an *odu* that symbolically addresses elements of the natural and social worlds, influencing personality traits, behaviors, physiognomy, and life events. *Odu* thus functions as an abstract intersection with axé, serving as a key element in Candomblé's spiritual framework.

Finally, Candomblé possesses few written texts and most mythic narratives and principles are passed down orally, only occasionally being written down and have been compiled mostly by scholars (Prandi, 2001). Those narratives to which we do have access, however, evoke the words of the French anthropologist, and later initiate, Roger Bastide, who wrote, that "Candomblé philosophy is not a barbarian philosophy, but a subtle thought that has not yet been deciphered" (Bastide, 1945, 134). As we will explore in the following sections, anthropologists have undertaken significant efforts to uncover the "subtle thought" expressed in the oral literature and ritual practices of Candomblé. However, despite these revealing insights into religious forms of life, philosophers have yet to give them sustained attention. It is high time we join our colleagues in the effort to do conceptual justice to these traditions.

## 2 Mythic Narratives and Candomblé's Supreme Being

More than two decades ago, Schilbrack (2002, 1) bemoaned the lack of attention given to the study of myths from a philosophical perspective. It was a rare endeavor at the time, even though one might assume that philosophy would be a natural domain for exploring myths. Unfortunately, this assumption has held true only in a few exceptional cases. However, in our context, we find ourselves without an alternative. Oral literature is a primary source, demanding our reliance on mythic narratives to engage philosophically with Afro-Brazilian religions. As Mikel Burley (2022) points out, myths encapsulate worldviews that can genuinely be considered philosophical. Thus, the philosophy of religion stands to gain significant enrichment by according these narratives consistent and thoughtful attention.

In this section, I will delve into some mythic narratives of the Yoruba-derived Nagô tradition of Candomblé to extract a set of attributes of this tradition's high god. I will present theological viewpoints regarding the Supreme Being of 'African Traditional Religion' (ATR) – more specifically, of the traditional religion of the Yoruba people – which will serve as a backdrop against which to contrast the myths to be examined. I will then present the primary creation myths of Candomblé, highlighting references to the tradition's high god. Lastly, I will scrutinize these myths to uncover insights into the nature of the Supreme Being and evaluate their alignment with the theological perspectives offered earlier. I will argue that Candomblé's Supreme Being, as portrayed in the mythic narratives, is a limited god. Further, I will posit that this portrayal accounts for the complete absence of a problem of evil within this tradition, and that the myths suggest the moral ambivalence of Candomblé's Supreme Being and high deities, as well as the world itself. In so doing, I aim to shed light on why certain philosophical dilemmas do *not* emerge within certain traditions, rather than trying to force them into the mold of classical problems formulated within the predominantly theistic framework of most philosophy of religion.

## 2.1 The Mythology of the *Orixás*

While Candomblé Queto,[7] also known as Nagô, is a tradition primarily rooted in Yoruba culture, it has also been influenced by Kardecist,[8] Catholic, and Amerindian elements. This tradition has been extensively studied by anthropologists, ethnologists, and sociologists, resulting in a wealth of ethnographic sources. In this section, I will focus on Nagô mythology, particularly as it is presented in classic compilations and studies by Juana Elbein dos Santos (1976/2012), Monique Augras (1983/2008), Pierre Verger (1985/2019), Reginaldo Prandi (2001), and José Beniste (2006).

Although there are no specific myths centered around the high god of Candomblé, Olorum (Ọlọ́run), also known as Olodumare (Olódùmarè),[9] this deity nevertheless plays a significant role in various Yoruba and Yoruba-derived myths, particularly those related to the origins of existence and the creation of the earthly realm, the *aiê* (*àiyé*). Before creation, only the spiritual realm, referred to as *orum* (*ọ̀run*) existed. Adebanji Akintoye (2010, 48) explains that

---

[7] The Brazilian Portuguese rendering of the Yoruba "Kétu" and synonymous with "Nagô" (from the Yoruba "Ànàgó"), originally referring to a subgroup of the Yoruba people mainly living in the town of Kétu (Kétou) in the Republic of Benin and southwest Yorubaland.

[8] Brazilian Kardecism, a transplant of nineteenth-century French Spiritism (founded by Allan Kardec), emphasizes mediumship for communicating with spirits and highlights healing, miracles, and the veneration of leaders renowned for their spiritual evolution. Kardecists believe in soul progression through multiple incarnations, guided by disincarnated souls, with charity as a central virtue (Engler and Isaia, 2016).

[9] The supreme being of Candomblé is perhaps most often referred to in Brazil as Olorum (Ọlọ́run, lit. "lord of the ọ̀run") but also Olodumare (Olódùmarè, possibly "owner of the source of creation"), the title most used in Yorubaland. Because the myths will use both names interchangeably, I have made the pedagogical choice to use the composite hyphenated "Olorum-Olodumare" to avoid confusion. I will also do this when mentioning *orixás* who are known by more than one name and who are central to the mythic narratives of Candomblé, namely, Oxalá-Obatalá and Orunmilá-Ifá.

at least since the tenth century CE, Yoruba mythology envisioned the spiritual realm as comprising two distinct spheres: a higher and a lower one. The higher sphere is where the supreme Olorum-Olodumare resides. The Yoruba people, in general, held the belief that humans could not fathom the types of sacrifices that would appease this high god. In contrast, the second heavenly sphere exists in close proximity to the earthly realm and serves as the abode for all other deities and ancestors, organized in a hierarchical order from the highest to the lowest.

By most accounts, the top tier includes the triad of Yoruba high deities: Oxalá (whose name is a contraction of Orixanlá, from Òrìṣànlá), also known as Obatalá (Ọbàtálá); Orunmilá (Ọ̀rúnmìlà), also known as Ifá; and Exu (Èṣù). In our exploration of the mythic narratives that revolve around Olorum-Olodumare, Oxalá-Obatalá takes center stage as the primary protagonist. He is credited with nothing less than the creation of the earthly world, and sometimes even all the beings that inhabit it. Orunmilá-Ifá, on the other hand, is the Yoruba deity associated with divination, knowledge, and wisdom. While not at the core of Candomblé worship, he plays a significant role in numerous mythic narratives. And, finally, there is Exu, who Augras (1983/2008, 91) describes as "the personification of the principle of transformation" and who some myths say was the first individual being created by Olorum-Olodumare.

Even if Olorum-Olodumare does inhabit the same plane of existence as the highest deities, Akintoye maintains that Olorum-Olodumare is supreme and unfathomable.[10] This aligns with Candomblé mythology and practice, since in Brazil, much like in Yorubaland, there are no shrines or sacrifices dedicated to Olorum-Olodumare (Carneiro, 1948/2019, 63). In fact, one might spend a considerable amount of time in a *terreiro* before hearing mention of Olorum-Olodumare unless one specifically inquires as to the world's creation, the origin of the *orixás*, or the ultimate source of *axé*. In that respect, the myths tell of a time when the spiritual and earthly realms were not separated.

## 2.2 The "God" of African Traditional Religion

Equating Olorum-Olodumare, the supreme being of Candomblé, with *God* – by which most Western philosophers usually think of the God of Abrahamic religions – is far from uncontroversial. While this matter is seldom debated among scholars in countries with significant Yoruba-diasporic religious communities, such as Brazil, Cuba, Haiti, and the Dominican Republic, in the context of African philosophy, discussions on this topic date back to the

---

[10]   Because Olorum-Olodumare is generally considered to be genderless or beyond human gender categories, I have respected this fact by avoiding gender-specific language, even while risking awkward sentence construction.

1960s. Furthermore, in recent years, these debates have drawn upon classic arguments in the philosophy of religion (Agada and Attoe, 2023).

In the past, African religious thinkers primarily focused on what Kwasi Wiredu (1998) referred to as the decolonization of African religion. Scholars such as Bọlajı Idowu (1962), John Mbiti (1970), Ọmọṣade Awolalu and Adelumo Dọpamu (1979), all possessing a Christian theological background, took it upon themselves to refute the racially biased arguments put forth by early European missionaries and anthropologists. Influential authors like the explorers Samuel Baker and Richard Burton had held a very negative view of ATR. Baker, for instance, declared that Africans "are without a belief in a Supreme Being, neither have they any form of worship or idolatry, nor is the darkness of their minds enlightened by even a ray of superstition" (cited in Ray (1976), 2). In his turn, Burton (1864, 199) claimed that "The Negro is still at the rude dawn of faith-fetishism, and he has barely advanced to idolatry ... He has never grasped the idea of a personal deity." As part of the post-colonial scholars' (very understandable) reactive attitude, running across their writings is the idea that, on the contrary, ATR is properly monotheistic. As such, Idowu and Mbiti, among others, espoused the view that the "God" of ATR is supreme, transcendent, creator, omnipotent, omniscient, and omnibenevolent. In short, the view that Olorum-Olodumare is what John Bishop (1998) has called an "omniGod." Let's call this view #1.

In their understandable fervor, however, they might have overcorrected. Scholars like Otok p'Bitek (1971) and Byang Kato (1975) have argued that those who were part of the first wave of the decolonization effort did not go as far as they should have in contesting the claims made by the likes of Baker and Burton. They suggest that those African scholars' Christian beliefs and agenda might have limited their ability to accurately interpret genuine African viewpoints on the Supreme Being of ATR. John Bewaji (1998, 4) goes so far as to accuse them of smuggling "their Christian beliefs into the religious terrain of Africa; they Hellenized and clothed the African God in borrowed garbs, as if He had always been nude." Nevertheless, the view that Yoruba religious thought warrants understanding Olorum-Olodumare in maximal theistic terms still finds adherents in contemporary scholars such as Ebunoluwa Oduwole (2007), who Ademola Fayemi (2012) accuses of making the same mistakes as the post-colonial scholars who, in their efforts to refute the claim that Africans lacked a coherent concept of God, allegedly integrated foreign categories into African religious thought. Fayemi argues that in Yoruba cosmogony, the Supreme Being is perceived as limited. Moreover, as we will see next, Fayemi (2012, 11) emphasizes that, unlike God in the Christian tradition, Olorum-Olodumare and the other deities are not considered perfect beings who cannot be malevolent.

Relying, like Bewaji and Fayemi do, on a critical examination of oral mythic narrative sources of African religious thought, Olusegun Oladipo (2004) also challenges the traditional theistic interpretation of Olorum-Olodumare and defends the idea of a limited god. As he observes, Yoruba mythology repeatedly depicts a Supreme Being who fashioned the world using preexisting materials – where "preexisting" can encompass notions of eternal existence, as well as antecedence to or coexistence with Olorum-Olodumare. The clear inference drawn from the assertion that the Supreme Being shaped the world from materials that perpetually existed is that Olorum-Olodumare possesses certain limitations, suggesting a departure from the traditional concepts of omnipotence and transcendence. Moreover, Oladipo (2004, 360) affirms that if we view omnipotence as the possession of infinite powers, it is questionable whether Olorum-Olodumare can be genuinely seen as all-powerful. Thus, Bewaji, Fayemi, and Oladipo all argue that the mythic narratives of the Yoruba imply that Olorum-Olodumare is supreme, but not transcendent; creator, but not omnipotent, omniscient, or omnibenevolent. Let's call this view #2.

Finally, another view is presented by Segun Gbadegesin (2013), who suggests that even the toned-down conception of Olorum-Olodumare proposed by view #2 goes too far. Gbadegesin argues that Yoruba belief recognizes other divinities with supreme authority in specific domains. For instance, Orunmilá-Ifá governs destiny, while Exu presides over order and balance. As these deities have a direct impact on human well-being, Gbadegesin contends that Olorum-Olodumare's centrality should be questioned, especially taking into consideration the lack of temples, rituals, or cults dedicated to Olorum-Olodumare in most of Yorubaland. According to Gbadegesin, Olorum-Olodumare should be viewed as the "first among equals" rather than unambiguously supreme. This perspective – let's call it view #3 – places Olorum-Olodumare in the same rank as Orunmilá-Ifá, Exu, and Oxalá-Obatalá, all of whom have authority and power over the world. Below this tier would be the other *orixás* (e.g., Oxum, Ogum, and Iemanjá), followed by the ancestors on a lower spiritual plane. Finally, beneath the spiritual realm, we find the earthly world inhabited by humans and other living beings. Because the most theologically significant narratives about Olorum-Olodumare's nature are found in the myths of creation of the *aiê*, we will look to three different sources to evince the attributes of Candomblé's high god.

## 2.3 Creation Stories

Elbein dos Santos (1976/2012, 59) provides us with one of the few narratives about what happened even before the emergence of the *orixás*, the creation of the earthly world, and its definitive separation from the spiritual world. She recounts:[11]

> [I]n the beginning, there was nothing but air; Ọlọrun was an infinite mass of air; when it began to move slowly, to breathe, part of the air turned into a mass of water, originating the great *Òrìṣà-Funfun*, *òrìṣà* of white. The air and water moved together and a part of themselves turned into mud. From this mud a bubble or mound emerged, the first matter to be given shape, a reddish and muddy rock. Ọlọrun admired this shape and blew on the mound, breathing his breath and giving it life. This form, the first endowed with individual existence, a laterite rock, was *Èṣù*, or rather, the proto-*Èṣù*, *Èṣù Yangí*. (Elbein dos Santos, 1976/2012, 61)

Thus, when Olorum-Olodumare decided to create the earthly world, he called on the great *orixá*, the firstborn, Oxalá-Obatalá, who the narrative earlier calls the "*orixá* of white" and the next one will call the "Lord of the White Cloth" (a literal translation of 'Ọbàtálá'). This begins what is probably the most widespread narrative of creation in Nagô mythology. There are various compilations of this myth in the literature and, having examined a wealth of extant sources, Prandi does a commendable job capturing its essence:

> In a time when the world was only Olodumare's imagination, there was only the infinite firmament and, beneath it, the vastness of the sea. Olorum, the Lord of Heaven, and Olocum, the Mistress of the Oceans, were of the same age and shared the secrets of what was and would be. Olorum and Olocum had two children: Orixalá, the firstborn, also called Obatalá, and Odudua, the youngest.
>
> Olorum-Olodumare entrusted Obatalá, the Lord of the White Cloth, with the creation of the world. [Olorum] bestowed powers upon him for this purpose. Obatalá sought the counsel of Orunmilá, who advised him to make offerings to succeed in the mission. But Obatalá did not take Orunmilá's prescriptions seriously, as he believed solely in his own powers. Odudua observed everything attentively and on that day, he also consulted Orunmilá. Orunmilá assured Odudua that if he made the prescribed sacrifices, he would become the ruler of the world that was to be created. The offering consisted of four hundred thousand chains, a chicken with five-toed feet, a pigeon, and a chameleon, along with four hundred thousand cowries. Odudua made the offerings.
>
> On the day of the creation of the world, Obatalá set out on a journey to the border of the beyond, where Exu is the guardian. Obatalá did not make the offerings in that place, as prescribed. Thus, a great thirst began to torment Obatalá. Obatalá approached a palm tree and touched its trunk with his long staff. Wine gushed abundantly from the palm tree and Obatalá drank from the wine until he became intoxicated. He became completely drunk and fell asleep on the road, under the shade of the palm tree. No one would dare to

---

[11] All translations from Portuguese and Spanish-language sources in this Element are my own.

awaken Obatalá. Odudua watched everything. When he was certain that Oxalá was asleep, Odudua picked up the sack of creation that had been given to Obatalá by Olorum. Odudua went to Olodumare and told him what had happened. Olodumare saw the sack of creation in Odudua's possession and entrusted him with the task of creating the world. Then Odudua took the chameleon and made it walk on that surface, demonstrating the firmness of the place. Obatalá was still asleep. Odudua set out for the Earth to claim it as his own.

Then, Obatalá woke up and learned of what had transpired. He returned to Olodumare and recounted his story. Olodumare said, "The world has already been created. You missed a great opportunity." To punish him, Olodumare forbade Obatalá from drinking palm wine forever, him and all his descendants. But the mission was not yet complete, and Olodumare bestowed another gift upon Obatalá: the creation of all living beings that would inhabit the Earth. And so, Obatalá created all living beings, and he created man and woman. Obatalá molded the human beings from clay, and the breath of Olodumare brought them to life. The world was now complete. And all praised Obatalá. (Prandi, 2001, 503–506)

An alternative telling of the myth of Oxalá-Obatalá and the creation of the earthly world, also compiled by Prandi (2001, 502–503), omits the participation of Odudua. Elbein dos Santos, who is one among other scholars who characterize Odudua as female, says that "The fight for the supremacy between the sexes is a constant factor in all Nagô myths" (1976/2012, 62–63). Importantly, this is a reminder that Candomblé myths are not univocal. Indeed, the alternative telling has Oxalá-Obatalá actually succeeding in singlehandedly creating the earthly world. This time, he does not ignore Orunmilá-Ifá's advice, so this alternative telling is less of a cautionary tale regarding the importance of offering and sacrifice (as well as never forgetting to appease Exu before one sets out to do something significant). While Prandi's version of the alternative telling does not feature Oxalá-Obatalá becoming inebriated with palm wine, the detailed version compiled by Beniste (2006) does – agreeing with other compilations of Yoruba mythology, such as Harold Courlander's (1973, 34–35). Yet, the consequence this time is not that Oxalá-Obatalá misses the opportunity to be the lord of creation, but that he mishandles a different task. As the following excerpt from Beniste's version tells us:

With all the elements in his power, Ọbàtálá completed the task, equipping the Earth with woods, forests, rivers, and waterfalls. Soon after, he was assigned another job, that of modeling the physical image of those who were to inhabit the entire created Earth. To do this, he turned the clay over and moistened it with water from the springs, modeling, in the form determined by Olódùmarè, figures identical to human beings. Ọbàtálá worked tirelessly, becoming exhausted and very thirsty. He sought to help himself with palm wine, *ẹmu*. Therefore, he went to look for liquid among the oil palm trees to alleviate his thirst. Upon extracting the liquid, he let it ferment and then drank it for a long time until he felt his body soften and everything around him spin. When he managed to stand up, he returned to work, but without his initial conditions. As a result, several models of the figures became clumsy, misshapen, with crooked legs and arms. ... Even so, everyone was placed in an appropriate position, awaiting the presence of the Supreme Being to give life to all the inanimate figures.

The instruction given to Ọbàtálá, therefore, was that, when he had completed his part in the creation of Man, he would notify Olódùmarè, who would then come to give life, placing the *ẹmìí*[12] in their bodies, thus completing the creation of the human being. From mere molded clay figures, they transformed into beings of blood, nerves, and flesh. With life breathed into their nostrils, they began to walk and do the things necessary for their survival.

When the effect of the palm wine ceased, Ọbàtálá saw that some humans he had molded were deformed. He was sad and felt remorse. Then he said, "I will never drink palm wine again. I will always be the protector of all humans who are defective or who were created imperfect." Because of this promise, human beings who are lame, blind, armless, deaf, mute, and those who have no pigment in their skin, albinos, are called *Ẹni Òrìṣà*, special people under his protection. (Beniste, 2006, 47–48)

Equipped with the aforementioned mythic narratives, which constitute the foundation of Nagô beliefs concerning Olorum-Olodumare, the creation of the earthly realm, and the dynamics between Olorum-Olodumare and the higher *orixás*, we are now adequately poised to evaluate the validity of the perspectives articulated by scholars of ATR in the context of the Supreme Being of Candomblé Nagô.

## 2.4 What the Myths Imply

With the exception of supremeness, which is only questioned by Gbadegesin, every other quality that view #1 attributes to Olorum-Olodumare is either contradicted by the narratives or cannot be inferred from them directly. As we have seen, Elbein dos Santos' (1976/2012, 61) account of the Yoruba myth of the origin of the universe tells that Olorum-Olodumare was originally an infinite mass of air a part of which, when it began to move and breathe, turned into a mass of water that gave rise to Oxalá-Obatalá. The movement of air and water then originated mud, which turned to rock, on which Olorum-Olodumare breathed life, creating Exu.

---

[12] Yoruba word meaning "breath," often extended to "life" and taken to be, along with *ori*, one of the aspects of the human soul. Rendered as *emi* in Portuguese.

Thus, Yoruba genetic myths support at least two arguments against transcendence. First, if Olorum-Olodumare created the world using preexisting materials, this implies that the Supreme Being has always been an integral part of the world order. Therefore, Olorum-Olodumare cannot be said to exist beyond the world. Second, Yoruba mythology repeatedly tells that Olorum-Olodumare resides in the *orum* and not beyond it. If Olorum-Olodumare's abode is within the *orum*, and the *orum* is part of the world, then Olorum-Olodumare cannot be said to exist outside the world. Furthermore, as we have seen, the myths tell of a time characterized by constant interaction between humans in the *aiê* and the spiritual beings in the *orum*, during which humans could visit Olorum-Olodumare's abode at their convenience.

The myths also do not warrant saying that Olorum-Olodumare's status as sole creator of the universe is unambiguous. Even if Olorum-Olodumare's action (or rather, movement) is responsible for the origination of the elements from which Oxalá-Obatalá, Exu, and plausibly the other *orixás* are engendered, Nagô mythology tells that the creation of the earthly world and the living beings that reside in it is either delegated to Oxalalá-Obatalá singlehandedly, or the task is split between Oxalá-Obatalá and Odudua. As Bewaji (1998, 8) notes, where Olorum-Olodumare did not directly cause or create, the orixás were nevertheless instructed and supervised by the Supreme Being (although the extent and competence of such supervision is questioned by some of the mythic narratives, such as Courlander's and Beniste's versions).

Ostensibly, to attribute the classical theist traits of omnipotence, omniscience, and omnibenevolence to Olorum-Olodumare is to go beyond the descriptive exercise of attempting to construct a picture from the mythic narratives and rather to venture into a normative theological exercise unconstrained by (and perhaps unconcerned with) the myths. As first evidence of this, note that nowhere in the Yoruba narratives or the Nagô myths derived from them does one ever hear that Olorum-Olodumare is an all-powerful, all-knowing, and all-good being. According to the myths, Olorum-Olodumare is indeed the source of all life and the source of all power (e.g., breathing life into a laterite rock to create Exu, breathing life into human shapes to engender humans, conferring power to the *orixás* to be creators, managers, protectors, and messengers). Moreover, Oxalá-Obatalá and the other *orixás* are either created by, or ultimately emerge from, Olorum-Olodumare. As the source of all life and the one who confers power to the *orixás* and delegates to them the creation and subsequent administration of the earthly world, we may infer from the myths that Olorum-Olodumare is the *most* powerful being, that is, supremely powerful, but not necessarily omnipotent.

The same goes for omniscience and omnibenevolence, of which there is no indication in the myths. In fact, the mythic narratives do not even imply that Olorum-Olodumare possesses the highest knowledge or moral goodness, let alone being perfectly or maximally knowledgeable or morally good. On the one hand, when it comes to omniscience, it is worth noting that in instances where knowledge is sought, such as at the outset of Oxalá-Obatalá's quest to create the earthly world, individuals turn to Orunmilá-Ifá, the deity of divination, rather than to Olorum-Olodumare. Interestingly, some Yoruba myths even depict Olorum-Olodumare seeking guidance from Orunmilá-Ifá (Bewaji, 1998, 8; Gbadegesin, 2013, 107). On the other hand, regarding omnibenevolence, the myths not only portray Olorum-Olodumare allowing evil to go unchallenged and uncorrected but also present Olorum-Olodumare as a distant and seemingly unempathetic persona. Furthermore, if the responsibility for the fact that the *orixás* themselves commit evil under Olorum-Olodumare's gaze can ultimately be traced back to the Supreme Being, this would imply that Olorum-Olodumare is morally ambivalent at best. This resonates with Bewaji (1998, 11), who affirms that the Supreme Being of Yoruba religion "is conceivable as capable of both good and bad" and "uses both for the ultimate good governance of the universe."

In that respect, recall that in Beniste's (2006, 47–48) narrative Olorum-Olodumare delegates the creation of human beings to Oxalá-Obatalá, who then gets intoxicated on palm wine while taking a respite from his toils and proceeds to craft compromised shapes, supposedly representing every congenital disability. Instead of correcting Oxalá-Obatalá's mistakes, or urging him to try again, Olorum-Olodumare decides to breathe life into these human forms, lending support to Bewaji when he states that Olorum-Olodumare "created both the good and the bad, the well-formed and the deformed [*sic*], the rainy season and the drought" (1998, 8). As co-creators, Olorum-Olodumare and Oxalá-Obatalá would seem to naturally share the responsibility for the evil that ensues from their negligence. However, while, in a poignant moment in Beniste's narrative, Oxalá-Obatalá vows to make amends for the wrongs he has committed, pledging to protect those who suffer due to his negligence, Olorum-Olodumare does and says nothing.

The theme of blame appears in a teaching story in Cuban Lucumí about Oddúa (the Caribbean Spanish rendering of Odùduwà) compiled by Natalia Aróstegui (1994). While Odudua is omitted from Beniste's version of the creation myth, Aróstegui recounts a narrative in which the *orixá* is enlisted to correct an actual mistake left by the Supreme Being (called Olofi in Afro-Caribbean religions of Yoruba descent, from *ǫlǫ*, meaning "owner" and *ǫfin*, "origin"):

> When Olofi wanted to create the world, he descended with Obatalá (this Obatalá is the oldest of them all, Obatalá-Occuá). With enthusiasm for

creation, Olofi made marvelous things (like the ceiba tree, the clouds, the rainbow, and the hummingbird), but he also faced failures and left some things unfinished. For instance, he left humans without heads. Naturally, they wandered directionless, and the world seemed like a madhouse. Annoyed, Olofi entrusted Oddúa to give them heads. Oddúa did so but left them with only one eye. It was Iba-Ibo who had to come and place their eyes where they are now and give them mouths, voices, and words. That's when humans began to be as we know them, and everything seemed fine. However, today, they threaten to disrupt all of Olofi's creation, and one doesn't know whether to blame the Father of the orishas or Oddúa, or whether to be sad or burst into laughter. (Aróstegui, 1994, 88)

Whether Olorum-Olodumare only orders Oxalá-Obatalá (or Odudua) to create and shape human beings or takes an active role in this creation and shaping – be it breathing life into the human forms or even co-creating and co-shaping them – it seems that Olorum-Olodumare would have both the power and the opportunity to correct the mistakes alluded to in Beniste's and Aróstegui's narratives. Why then is it that the problem of evil does not naturally arise in Yoruba and Yoruba-influenced religions? The fact that view #1 is contradicted by the myths makes sense of this absence when we look at the general structure of the problem as it is understood by contemporary philosophers. For instance, Michael Hickson (2013, 16) summarizes it as follows: if there is a God, then God must possess attributes X, Y, or Z; but evil shows that God cannot possess attributes X, Y, or Z; therefore, there is no God.

Hickson's summary directs our attention to the fact that arguments from evil are specifically aimed at undermining modern proponents of perfect-being theology, the core of which is the omniGod thesis (Nagasawa, 2008). The arguments usually come in two forms. The logical problem of evil is the appearance of inconsistency between the existence of God and the existence of any evil at all, such that a defense against it is thus an argument that aims to show that this appearance is misleading. On the other hand, the evidential problem of evil focuses on the inconsistency of maximal-person properties and gratuitous, horrendous evil (not just any evil). A common example that chimes with our previous discussion is that of a child born with severe and painful congenital disorders. Here is a paraphrase of William Rowe's (1979, 336) original formulation of the argument:

1. Gratuitous, horrendous evil sometimes occurs, which an omnipotent, omniscient, and omnibenevolent being could prevent without sacrificing a greater good or allowing equally terrible evil.

2. An omnipotent, omniscient, and omnibenevolent being would prevent gratuitous, horrendous evil, when possible, unless doing so would result in the loss of a greater good or the allowance of equally severe evil.
3. An omnipotent, omniscient, and omnibenevolent being does not exist.

The argument thus examines the world to identify elements in our experiences that may cast doubt on the existence of an omniGod and then points to the existence of intense, seemingly unwarranted human and animal suffering as one such element. Based on this observation, Rowe contends that the existence of an omniGod is highly improbable, providing reasonable grounds for embracing atheism, which in this case means rejecting classical, personalist theism. However, if Olorum-Olodumare is not an omniGod, the problem of evil becomes irrelevant. Oladele Balogun (2009, 15) agrees, noting that the Yoruba perspective on Olorum-Olodumare as a high god makes it impossible for this Supreme Being to possess absolute attributes like all-powerfulness, all-knowingness, and all-goodness that give rise to the philosophical problem of evil. Since arguments from evil target the existence of an omniGod, the rejection of view #1 clarifies why Candomblé does not grapple with the problem. Candomblé does not adhere to perfect-being theology. Olorum-Olodumare is not an omniGod.

Finally, considering the significance of Oxalá-Obatalá, Orunmilá-Ifá, and Exu, there lingers a final question: is Olorum-Olodumare truly the Supreme Being in Candomblé, or does view #3, suggesting that Olorum-Olodumare is merely the first among equals, hold more merit? While the myths may portray Oxalá-Obatalá as more benevolent than Olorum-Olodumare, while emphasizing Orunmilá-Ifá's supreme knowledge, and underscoring Exu's indispensable role in all endeavors, view #3 is contradicted by the fact that Olorum-Olodumare is everywhere depicted as the origin of everything and the bestower of life and *axé*. Thus, Olorum-Olodumare *is* the Supreme Being in Candomblé, despite occasional dependence on Oxalá-Obatalá, Orunmilá-Ifá, and Exu. Still, a more in-depth exploration of the myths may offer a basis for further discussion, potentially leading to more debate on the choice between views #2 and #3, or even the emergence of an alternative perspective. Further engaging in this speculative exploration, which honors the mythic narratives, would be a welcome instance of a narrative turn in the philosophy of religion and it would add to the exploration of neglected forms of religiosity that extend well beyond the typical Western philosophical concerns.

Writing in the 1940s, the eminent Brazilian anthropologist Edison Carneiro foreshadowed the African scholars who would, from the 1960s on, defend ATR from its relegation to fetishism or, at the very least, polytheism. Carneiro declared with assurance that:

> We now know that in them [Afro-diasporic religions], the existence of a being was always admitted, whom the Yoruba called Olorum (a word that means Lord or Owner of Heaven) and whom the Bantu-speaking Africans called Zâmbi or Zambiampungo (which eventually became Zaniapombo in Brazil). All the qualities of the gods in universal religions, such as Christianity and Islam, are attributed to the supreme divinity, who has no altars, organized worship, and cannot be materially represented. (Carneiro, 1948/2019, 14)

While this type of homogenizing judgment may be well-intentioned, the oral mythic narratives transmitted across generations by Candomblé practitioners offer a contrasting perspective. Even if we avoid taking these narratives too literally and acknowledge their multifaceted nature, they function as a linguistic instrument for articulating the values, beliefs, and commitments of religious communities – aspects that history, and perhaps even ethnographic fieldwork, may not entirely unveil. In the absence of universally agreed-upon codified texts, these narratives become invaluable resources for us to, within the realm of philosophy of religion, approach these overlooked traditions with due respect. An additional facet of our endeavor to comprehend the worldview, which is equally essential, will require a closer examination of ritual practices, aided by ethnography – a resource that philosophers of religion have, regrettably, overlooked for far too long. Ideally, philosophizing by immersing ourselves in myths and rituals should encompass an appreciation of the complexities and richness inherent in these forms of life, free from the imposition of external philosophical assumptions or biases. However, it is important to recognize that, at times, doing conceptual justice to a religious form of life will entail showing differences rather than seeking commonalities, and that is entirely acceptable.

## 3 Sacrifice and the Indispensability of Ethnography

As argued by Douglas Hedley in a recent study, sacrifice is "a universal component of the human imaginary" (2011, 2). Despite this, sacrifice remains an elusive concept, challenging both to define and explain, and largely overlooked within the realm of philosophy of religion, with rare exceptions (Burley, 2020, ch. 6). Over a century ago, Henri Hubert and Marcel Mauss (1899) described sacrifice as a religious practice, highlighting how the sanctification of a victim reshapes the moral disposition of practitioners and infuses certain ritual objects with new significance. Both literal and metaphorical forms of sacrifice – such as the sacrifice of personal desires for the benefit of others – yield transformative outcomes, impacting not only the community but also individual practitioners. While Hubert and Mauss's framework focuses on the fundamental aspects of sacrifice rather than offering functionalist explanations, subsequent theories often fall into two categories: sacrifice as an exchange or consumption economy, and sacrifice as catharsis (Flood, 2013). Despite their differences, these theories share an approach centered on understanding the cultural function of sacrifice.

While the prevalence and maintenance of animal sacrifice in Afro-Brazilian religions is often treated as exotic, there are numerous examples of similar practices in mainstream religious traditions that support the point that sacrifice is spread globally and that it is still a prototypical feature of religious practice. For instance, while contemporary Hinduism typically avoids it, exceptions persist in regions like Eastern India and Nepal. Sacrifices involving goats, chickens, and water buffaloes are notable during celebrations like the Gadhimai festival, attracting millions of devotees. These rituals, honoring deities like Durga and Kali, seek their favor and serve to appease their wrath (Fuller, 2004). Similarly, *qurbān*, or *uḍhiya*, remains a significant Islamic ritual, commemorating Prophet Ibrahim's obedience to Allah's command. Muslims worldwide perform sacrificial slaughter during Eid al-Adha, dividing the meat to share with family, friends, and the less fortunate (Banerjee, 2021, ch. 5).

The examination of blood sacrifice is all but absent in the philosophy of religion. This absence raises the questions of how philosophy of religion can benefit from ethnographic material and crudely put, of what business philosophy has in describing religious forms of life and probing for the meaning of its rituals. As Burley notes, "it is not immediately obvious how to utilize this material in philosophically productive ways. In large part, this is because of the paucity of existing discussions of phenomena such as animal sacrifice and divine possession in the philosophical literature" (2023, 187). Notably, previous philosophical encounters with blood sacrifice offer little guidance.

Burley points to John Hick, John Stewart, and Douglas Hedley as rare instances where philosophers have addressed animal sacrifice, however briefly and dismissively – viewing such practices as outdated customs surpassed by the "major" religions. For instance, Hick categorizes Vedic religion, specifically its practice of ritual sacrifice, as belonging to "pre-axial" religions (Hick, 2004, 27) – that is, those that still bear the mark of a phase in human history characterized by less sophisticated philosophical and religious thought, lacking the depth and complexity observed since the "axial age" (c. 800–200 BCE). In his turn, Stewart characterizes animal sacrifice as appearing "quaint and economically ill-advised" from a contemporary perspective (Stewart, 2008, 110). Even Hedley, in his astute exploration of sacrifice, glosses over "sacrifice in the strict ritual sense" as a religious element primarily associated with "ancient or archaic societies" (2011, 2). This tendency not only ignores the continued prevalence of animal sacrifice today, especially in cultures often neglected by philosophers of religion, but also disregards the central role these practices play in various religious forms of life.

In this section, my aim is not to advocate for any particular theory of sacrifice. Instead, I seek to explore the meaning of sacrifice within Afro-Brazilian traditions. Drawing insights from ethnographic studies, I aim to begin elucidating the network of emic concepts essential for understanding sacrifice's significance within these traditions – starting from the division between the *aiê* and the *orum*, which gives rise to the need for the primary ritual practices. To explore why sacrifice, and particularly why blood sacrifice, is deemed necessary, I will continue to draw from mythic narratives and then transition to ethnographies, which will continue to inform subsequent explorations of initiation, possession, material culture, and embodiment. After presenting the narrative origins of the practice of sacrifice, I will delve into the meaning of spilling blood for the acquisition and transference of *axé*, and then examine a specific sacrificial ritual, the *bori* – a gateway to initiation. I conclude this section with a brief reflection on ethnographically informed philosophy of religion and what it entails.

## 3.1 The Mythic Origins of Candomblé Rituals

In the following mythic narrative, prevalent especially in Nagô *terreiros* in Recife and Rio de Janeiro, Prandi gives an account of the origin of the key practices of sacrifice, initiation, and possession.

> In the beginning, there was no separation between the Orum, the Heaven of the *orixás*, and the Aiê, the Earth of humans. Humans and deities came and went, living together and sharing lives and adventures. It is said that, when the Orum bordered the Aiê, a human being touched the Orum with dirty hands. The immaculate heaven of the Orixá had been defiled. The pristine whiteness of Obatalá was lost. Oxalá complained to Olorum. Olorum, the Lord of Heaven, the Supreme God, angered by the filth, waste, and carelessness of mortals, blew with divine wrath, and forever separated Heaven from Earth. Thus, the Orum was separated from the world of humans, and no one could go to the Orum and return from there alive. The *orixás* also could not come to Earth with their bodies. Now there was the world of humans and the world of *orixás*, apart. Isolated from the human inhabitants of the Aiê, the deities grew sad. The *orixás* longed for their escapades among humans, and they walked around in sadness and sulked. They went to complain to Olodumare, who eventually consented that the *orixás* could occasionally return to Earth. However, for this to happen, they would have to take on the material bodies of their devotees. This was the condition set by Olodumare.

Oxum, who used to delight in coming to Earth to play with women, sharing her beauty and vanity with them, teaching them spells of lovable seduction and irresistible charm, received a new task from Olorum: to prepare mortals to receive the *orixás* in their bodies. Oxum made offerings to Exu to facilitate her delicate mission. The joy of her fellow orixá siblings and friends depended on her success. She came to the Aiê and gathered women around her, bathing their bodies with precious herbs, cutting their hair, shaving their heads, and painting their bodies. She painted their heads with small white dots, like the feathers of the guinea fowl. She dressed them in beautiful fabrics and abundant bows, adorning them with jewelry and crowns. (...) Finally, the little brides were made,[13] they were ready, and they were *odara*.[14] The *iaôs*[15] were the most beautiful brides that Oxum's vanity could imagine. They were ready for the gods. The *orixás* now had their horses,[16] they could safely return to the Aiê, they could ride the bodies of the devotees. Humans made offerings to the *orixás*, inviting them to Earth, into the bodies of the *iaôs*. Thus, the *orixás* would come and mount their horses. And while the men played their drums, resonating the *batás* and *agogôs*, sounding the *xequerês* and *adjás*,[17] while the men sang, cheered, and applauded, inviting all initiated humans to the circle of *xirê*,[18] the *orixás* danced and danced and danced. The *orixás* could once again coexist with mortals. The *orixás* were happy. In the circle of those who were made, within the bodies of the *iaôs*, they danced and danced and danced. Candomblé had been created. (Prandi, 2001, 526–528)

The universe is thus conceptualized as having porous boundaries and is characterized by distinct levels wherein humans, ancestors, and deities engage in reciprocal interactions. Ancestral spirits and deities play pivotal roles in shaping human destinies, necessitating ceremonies to uphold harmonious relationships with them. Candomblé's integrated cosmology places the connection between the human realm and the *orixás*' world at its core, and what unites all entities in the universe is *axé* (Schmidt, 2024). *Axé* manifests in specific places such as riverbeds, quarries, and woods; objects such as stones, tools, fruits, and seeds;

---

[13] The Portuguese words for "made" ("feita(s)" in the feminine, "feito(s)" in the masculine) carry special significance since initiation is called *feitura* (lit. 'making').

[14] Yoruba-derived word meaning "good" and, by extension, "beautiful" widely used in Bahia, particularly in Candomblé circles, made widespread by Caetano Veloso's homonymous song.

[15] Yoruba-derived word meaning "young spouse," usually a female initiate of a lower rank in the initiatory journey of those who enter into possession trance, but also used to refer to male initiates.

[16] In Afro-Brazilian religions, the term "cavalo" (horse) symbolically denotes an initiated individual who can be possessed (or "mounted") by a particular *orixá* (or other spiritual entity), facilitating communication and interaction between the spiritual and human realms.

[17] Rhythmic instruments used in Afro-Brazilian rituals with the purpose of summoning the *orixás* or to induce possession trance. *Batá* is a type of drum commonly used in Xangô de Pernambuco; *agogô* is a double bell and one of the oldest instruments used in samba; *xerequê* is a rattle made with a gourd covered by a net of beads; and *adjá* is a small metal bell.

[18] Yoruba-derived word meaning "play" or "feast," it denotes a ritual in which initiates sing and dance in a circle for all the *orixás*.

and bodily parts, such as hearts, livers, lungs, and genitals (Léo Neto *et al.*, 2009, 3). Akin to matter, *axé* is indestructible and cannot be created, but is rather transmitted – "among objects, people, and *orixás*" (Seligman, 2014, 33).

Note that in the whole of the splendid mythology of the *orixás* compiled by Prandi, the word "*axé*" appears only a few times, disproportionately if one considers how ubiquitous it is in the speech of practitioners of Afro-Brazilian religions. When it does appear, however, it aligns with everyday discourse and ethnographic descriptions: it is a "vital force that transforms the world" (2001, 564), the "constructive power" (2001, 550) and "beneficent force of the *orixás*" (2001, 348). Yet, because the theme of ritual practices of sacrifice is only gleaned through mythic narratives, we must turn to ethnography and cultural anthropology for enriched descriptions and interpretations with which we can situate their meaning in the religious forms of life manifested by these traditions.

## 3.2 *Axé* and the Necessity of Spilling Blood

In Candomblé, all entities, be they inanimate, living, or spiritual, are seen, to different degrees, as enchanted beings (*encantados*). As Arno Vogel and colleagues (1993) observe, the key distinction lies in the various masks they wear, concealing the common primordial and divine essence from which they ultimately came from, namely, the supreme Olorum-Olodumare. As the mythic narrative earlier elucidates, this shared enchantment unites all of creation in a tragic dimension, marked by the separation between the world of deities and the world of creatures. Candomblé thus posits the need for sacrifice to reestablish a connection between the realm of individualized existence in the *aiê* and the domain of generic existence in the *orum*. "In the act of sacrifice, it draws upon all the components of this enchanted world" (Vogel *et al.*, 1993, 26).

In this way, *axé* can be replenished through fulfilling obligations (*obrigações*) to the *orixás*, the greatest bearers of *axé* with whom humans can come into contact, even if indirectly. The human body and the person are seen as vehicles and receptacles of *axé*, and periodically observing dietary and clothing restrictions, participating in ceremonies, as well as carrying out certain rituals enables its acquisition and renewal. Seligman refers to this process as "spiritual investment," involving material contributions, particularly offerings that serve as conduits for the transmission of *axé* between deities and humans.

> Many Candomblé ritual practices operate under the same principle of making links to the spiritual world through the material. Material offerings and behaviors serve to please and feed the deities, while at the same time bringing some *axé*, or spiritual force, to human beings. Such practices are

thus a means of materializing the spiritual power of the supernatural for the benefit of humans, in order to improve the earthly lives of adherents. (Seligman, 2014, 78)

Accordingly, investing in a connection with the deities through material offerings yields tangible outcomes, such as enhanced social connections, employment prospects, and this-worldly healing. Emphasizing such healing aspects, Gomberg (2011) characterizes the ritual obligations to the *orixás* as remedies for treating illnesses, potentially culminating in initiation into the community. Bettina Schmidt (2024) observes that in Candomblé the concept of well-being is intricately tied to maintaining a proper balance of *axé*, extending beyond mere physical health. While the individual has indeed the responsibility to live in a correct way, it is the obligations toward the ancestors and *orixás* that characterize how to live a good life, since the individual is part of a wider community that includes "other-than-human persons" (Hallowell, 1960). At the same time, shared rituals in which mediums incorporate the *orixás* contribute, as Seligman (2014, 133) notes, "an embodied dimension to the way in which they bring the rest of the community closer to the *axé* – helping laypeople to really feel the presence of this powerful force."

Blood is the main carrier of *axé* in any living being and is therefore the most important offering. As Roberto Motta (1991, 70) observes, the *axé* of spilled blood is considered the ultimate *axé*, representing the primary wellspring of life, energy, strength, health, and integrity. It signifies sustenance and is the quintessential source of holiness intricately intertwined with everyday existence. Robson Rogério Cruz, both a *babalorixá*[19] and an anthropologist, agrees and elaborates:

> In this specific case [sacrifice], the blood aligns with *axé*, signifying a unique connection. This particular blood-*axé* holds special significance, as the life force circulating through the body sustains its vitality. It implies that in every living being, including animals and ourselves, the life force originated from the divine touch we received, the *emi* from Olodumare. Therefore, the blood being shed in that moment embodies the presence of the creator. Essentially, this living blood possesses the potential for creation. This underscores its fundamental role in Candomblé rituals, where the creative essence of blood takes center stage. (Cruz, 2018)

Relaying her fieldwork in *terreiros* in São Paulo, Schmidt (2024) notes that in the ritual sacrifice presented on altars to the *orixás*, every animal becomes sacred, extending this status even to the dishes and bowls holding the offerings.

---

[19] In Candomblé, the spiritual leaders of a *terreiro* are known as *ialorixá* (lit., *orixá*-mother), synonymous with *mãe-de-santo* (mother-of-saint), or *babalorixá* (*orixá*-father), synonymous with *pai-de-santo* (father-of-saint).

The blood, along with parts of the animals deemed especially rich in *axé* (such as the head), is collected and placed on the altar. "No blood can be shed in vain as every drop contains *axé*," she observes. Emphasizing the significance of blood further underscores *axé* as a crucial element in safeguarding well-being. Any imbalance can lead to physical, mental, and even social disruption. As Schmidt avers, in the Candomblé worldview, living is a reciprocal relationship grounded in the interchange of *axé*.

### 3.3 Feeding the Head

Although offerings are primarily offered to deities, consider the following excerpt from a Yoruba-derived myth which more fully describes the practice of offering or *ebó*:

> There was a woman with a lot of problems (...) She went to consult the cowrie shells to know what to do. She was told to make an offering to the *ori*, her head. She was told to make a *bori*, she should feed her head. To her head the woman should offer two *obis*.[20] She then took the two *obis* and went to make the offering. (Prandi, 2001, 481–482)

This narrative provides an insight into a crucial legacy of Yoruba tradition that endures in contemporary Candomblé practices, namely, the primacy of *ori*, the individual and unique principle representing the head of each person, which holds sway over the fate of every mortal. As Augras (1983, 62) notes, "Even before offering a sacrifice to the deities, each person must make an offering to their own head." Thus, before initiation, a ritual sacrifice called *bori* takes place – literally an offering (*ebó*) to the head (*ori*). In a richly detailed ethno-graphic account of *bori*, Miriam Rabelo (2011, 16ff.) relays that, beginning at night, participants, whether leading or experiencing the *bori*, gather on stools or mats, and their heads are cleansed with a fragrant decoction of fresh leaves. The ritual proceeds with a series of offerings to the head, notably the *obi*, mentioned in the mythic narrative earlier. Boiled white corn, blood from a sacrificed pigeon, and *obi* slices are carefully positioned on the head and gathered in a basin held on each person's lap. They are presented with a sliver of *obi* to chew, and the resultant chips are spat into the priestess' hands, eventually being placed on the head. Subsequently, a white cloth band is secured around the head.

After the *bori*, those who underwent the ritual recline on mats wrapped in blankets, spending the night and a significant part of the next day in restful repose while indulging in foods associated with the *ori*, predominantly fruits. Throughout this period, they warmly welcome visiting members of the *terreiro*,

---

[20]  *Obi* refers to the Cola nut, an African fruit acclimatized in Brazil (*Cola acuminata, Streculiacea*).

generously share the fruits, and engage in conversation. It is not uncommon for some members of the house to undergo possession by their *orixás* when visiting those who underwent the *bori*. As nightfall approaches, the priestess finally brings the *bori* to a close, carefully untying the cloth band securing the food offerings, collecting the corn grains in a basin, and cleansing the saint-children's[21] heads with water. Following a refreshing bath, they receive instructions on behavioral and dietary practices for their protection – signifying the conclusion of the ritual.

Cruz (2003, 3) explains that the *ori* has two aspects, one physical and the other transcendental. One is the aspect responsible for thought and the senses; the other is the aspect that houses ancestry and mystical identity: "*eledá*, the individual *orixá*, who can later transform into a saint, with *feitura* [initiation]." Through strengthening these two forms, the individual becomes stronger as a whole. To this end, it is essential for practitioners to pay homage to their own heads. As an elder relayed to Ligia Barros Gama during a *bori*, "There are people who think that [*bori*] is to feed the *orixá*, but it's not! [*Bori*] is to feed the head" (Gama, 2009, 67). However, even if offering is seen as necessary, and blood is taken to be the most significant and *axé*-rich offering one can present, there still lingers the question of why an animal should die in the process – as presumably a blood sacrifice would not be impossible without the actual death of the animal. Cruz (1995) answers that initiation constitutes a total model of ritual restitution and rescue, and so needs to begin with the symbolic death of the postulant, and for someone to die and be reborn as another without the intermediation of their own physical death, there must occur the death of a third party.

> It is the much-feared "head swap". There is, in Candomblé, the belief that mothers- and fathers-of-saint reach advanced ages by postponing their own death by magically directing it to another person. In the process, the death of the *iaô* is transferred to that of the sacrificed quadruped (goat or sheep). The sacrifice of initiation is one of the few of which no testimony is kept. The remains of the dead animals, all the perishable elements used, and even the hair trimmed from the *iaô*'s head are dispatched, as they represent a burden of death. The aforementioned danger represented by the presence of initiated inmates in a house lies precisely in the proximity of death embodied by the transition. By dispatching the burden of their own death, the initiate nullifies its existence. Once reborn from death, a path of infinite life opens before them. (Cruz, 1995, 63)

The primary purpose of the *bori* ritual is thus to nourish the deified head and unleash *axé* by employing the blood derived from the sacrificial act

---

[21] In Candomblé, novices are referred to as *filha-de-santo* (saint-daughter) or *filho-de-santo* (saint-son), or by the Yoruba-derived term *abiã*, once they have completed the *ebó* and *bori* rituals.

performed on animals sanctified through this very act and for this very purpose. Elaborating on the significance of sacrifice as a primordial part of initiation, *babalorixá* Altair Bento de Oliveira (2009, 51) argues that the purpose of blood sacrifice lies in the transfer of the life of animals to the sacred object, passing through the *ori* to establish the close connection between the *ori*, the incorporated *orixá* – who, from that moment on, becomes a physical representation of the *orixá* – and the *orixá*'s altar, where they should from now on be worshiped. Therefore, the sacrifice does not promote benefit only individually but collectively, where there is an exchange of the animal's *axé* for the person and for the community, as *babalorixá* Agenor Miranda da Rocha also emphasizes:

> The blood of sacrificed animals in contact with people's heads allows a union of the three forces: orixá, *ori*, and person, forming a great chain, which interconnects all the components of the [community] and the *orixás* with each other. This meeting renews the *axé* of the house. Within this perspective, each person in the [community] is important and the well-being of each one becomes fundamental to the well-being of the others. (Rocha, 2000, 96)

In this sense, *axé* serves as both content and container (Wafer, 1991, 18). As content, it embodies the spiritual essence of Candomblé, contained within the ritual objects, people, spaces, foods, and practices of the religion. As container, it represents the ethos or broader circle encompassing the entire community, with those affiliated with the *terreiro* included within its *axé* to varying degrees. *Axé* as container "is like an organism defined by and sustaining itself by means of the circulation of its animating force," which is *axé* as content (Wafer, 1991, 19).

When the *bori* is concluded, the future brothers and sisters are invited to dance and welcome the head, saluting it in front of the mat. In hierarchical order, from the "oldest" to the "youngest," everyone will greet and wish health, *axé*, and prosperity to the new brother or sister (Gomberg, 2011, 154–155). The community's participation in the *bori* brings to the fore the view that the community is attentive to the health and well-being of those who frequent the *terreiro*, establishing actions of cooperation and solidarity in the various stages that will make up this procedure – from the acquisition of elements for the ritual to their eventual dispatch.

As Gomberg relays, in the aftermath of the *bori*, some people report experiencing a feeling that can be described as a mixture of relief, relaxation, and apprehension, in addition to the expectation of being aware that this ritual is the "gateway to the House" (Gomberg, 2011, 155), that is, the beginning of the individual's insertion and religious trajectory in the community – the last step before religious initiation itself, or "making the saint". In Section 4, we will look more closely at *feitura* and what it means for the construction of the identity not only of the initiate but also of the *orixá*.

## 3.4 Ethnographically Informed Philosophy of Religion

By looking at ritual sacrifice in Candomblé through engaging ethnographic fieldwork and cultural anthropology, I have endeavored to begin to situate their meaning in the forms of life of their practitioners. As we have seen, beyond the mythic origins of the need for offering, and blood sacrifice in particular, the Candomblé worldview presents a network of concepts and related practices revolving around *axé*. As we will see next, this fundamental concept is also profoundly connected with the creative process, or "making," that will result in the forging and finding of ritual objects, the individualization of *orixás*, and the construction of initiates' personhood. To do so, I will continue to rely on ethnographies of Afro-Brazilian religious rituals, not only because I must, but because ethnography allows for the exploration of religious aspects that resist straightforward summarization in conventional religious or philosophical texts. As Burley maintains (2023, 182–183), ethnography achieves this by revealing facets of "everyday," "lived," or "living" religion that are often overlooked in studies limited to non-ethnographic published materials.

In arguing that traditional philosophy of religion often employs descriptions that oversimplify or strip away the richness of religious experiences and practices, Knepper (2013) observes that these descriptions focus solely on doctrinal beliefs or abstract philosophical arguments, neglecting the lived experiences and cultural expressions of religion. Thus, as part of his suggestions for a "global-critical" philosophy of religion, in addition to formal comparison and critical evaluation, Knepper calls for "thick description," a term that Clifford Geertz adopted from two essays published by Gilbert Ryle in 1966 and 1968 (Ryle, 2009, chs. 36 and 37). Geertz found a compelling example in Ryle's work to elucidate the nature of this description. Ryle presented a scenario involving the rapid closing and reopening of someone's eye, offering two distinct possibilities: in one, the eye's movement was an involuntary twitch, lending itself to a concise description as a mere bodily motion; in the other case, the eye movement was a deliberate wink, intended to convey a message. Describing this deliberate wink required more than just detailing the bodily movement; it was, as Geertz observed, a meaningful "gesture" (Geertz, 1973, 6). Ryle (2009, ch. 37) went on to introduce additional layers of complexity to the possible scenarios. For instance, someone might entertain friends by humorously mimicking another person's conspiratorial wink. To perfect this mimicry, repeated practice might be involved. Describing this practice necessitated a description that was adverbially thick, akin to a sandwich with multiple layers.

However, in the ethnographic context, researchers often struggle to grasp the actions of those they study, necessitating consideration of various contextual factors, including individuals' perspectives. While these perspectives may not differ logically, incorporating multiple viewpoints enriches descriptions akin to the layered quality of sounds in a choir or a bustling cocktail party. Geertz underscores that situations involving multiple agents yield diverse interpretations, driving thick description, where the ethnographer constructs a nuanced understanding drawing from available data, including agents' interpretations. Ethnography thus becomes a fundamentally interpretive endeavor, unveiling layers of meaning, as Geertz illustrates with the metaphor of "winks upon winks upon winks" (Geertz, 1973, 9). Thus, Burley (2020, 62) concludes that Geertz's adoption of thick description can be seen as an extension or recontextualization of Ryle's original concept.

To achieve an ethnographically informed philosophy of religion with the guiding purpose of doing conceptual justice to the phenomena under investigation, the descriptive enterprise should remain open to the multiple 'dimensions of the sacred' (Smart, 1996), including the ritual, mythic, experiential, ethical, legal, social, material, and political in addition to the explicitly doctrinal aspects that have been the almost sole object of the philosophy of religion. For this purpose, philosophers can and should effectively employ existing sources that provide descriptively thick portrayals of religious experiences and practices. These include not only oral literature and ethnographic accounts, as Burley (2023, 181) notes, but also novels, plays, and films, as well as biographical or autobiographical works.

In its early stages, like other interdisciplinary methodologies, integrating research findings with existing literature poses a challenge. In this instance, as we will explore in the next two sections, there are opportunities to connect with ecological psychology and cognitive anthropology, but fewer connections to traditional philosophy of religion. To address this gap, I follow Burley's lead by emphasizing the hermeneutical and phenomenological aspects of philosophical inquiry. This involves seeking a descriptive account that is both evocative and conceptually nuanced, capable of challenging prevailing assumptions in the philosophy of religion. Such an approach is not only descriptive but also *critically* descriptive, as it disrupts common expectations and guards against overgeneralization (Burley, 2023, 184), while examining the meaning of practices and their ontological and epistemological significance.

As Schmidt (2024, 16) rightly contends, Candomblé offers a nuanced perspective on the world, blending material and spiritual dimensions in a manner that diverges from the commonly discussed religious and philosophical ideas in the Western context. This unique worldview serves as a means to enhance our philosophical comprehension of religion, as it destabilizes and defamiliarizes our own ingrained cultural assumptions. As Burley (2020, 59) emphasizes, this form of strong critique, achieved through cross-cultural comparison, not only challenges our assumptions about our own cultural values and practices but also prompts a reevaluation of those of the other culture involved in the comparison. It is thus evident that to adequately address the intricate and diverse nature of religion within a truly global philosophy of religion, employing thickly descriptive and ethnographically informed philosophical inquiry stands out as a promising approach to advancing this goal.

## 4 Objects, Ontology, and Personhood

In the last decade of the nineteenth century, Raymundo Nina Rodrigues, a foundational figure in Brazilian anthropology, observed a curious phenomenon: among the Black population of Bahia, everyday objects like stones and pieces of iron, once consecrated, were revered as deities. Rodrigues noted, "Any iron object can be revered as Ogum, provided it undergoes consecration" (1935, 43–44). This blending of deity and object led Rodrigues to coin the term "fetishist animism," describing it as a stage where gods possessed anthropomorphic traits yet retained the external forms of primitive fetishism (1935, 173). Over a century later, this perplexing fusion of objects and deities continues to intrigue scholars of Afro-Brazilian religions. Although often overlooked in favor of social, political, or economic dimensions, the ontological dynamics of Candomblé objects and how they not only stand for, but somehow mesh with persons and deities, has received much attention in recent anthropological scholarship, but has not been taken up by philosophers of religion. To begin correcting this oversight, in this section and in Section 5, we will look at how the *orixás* – often called "saints" in their individuated existence – make themselves present: first, in their material seat or settlement,[22] and, following initiation, in the body of the initiate, through possession. These are very different manifestations, but both are essential to the establishment of the relationship between the orixá and the initiate that will ultimately "make" them both. Indeed, this section will be devoted to this perhaps most important of verbs in the Afro-Brazilian religious jargon – *fazer* (to make) – and its ontological presuppositions and consequences.

---

[22] Although typically translated as "settlement," in Afro-Brazilian religions the *ibá* or *assentamento* is a shrine that serves both as a habitation and a seat (*assento*) to *orixás* and other entities. For our purposes, the Portuguese words *assentamento* and *assento*, as well as the Yoruba-derived *ibá*, should be taken as synonyms.

In this section, I will demonstrate how in the sort of world conceived of by Candomblé practitioners – abundant with *axé* – there is held to be the perpetual potential for creation, shaping energies toward specific ends, and enacting rituals imbued with significance. To begin elucidating the Candomblé view of the creative process, I will first present the practice of tool-making to show how this idea of creation diverges from the *ex-nihilo* model proposed by Judeo-Christian cosmologies. Afro-Brazilian creative processes involve realizing inherent potentialities within beings and objects in the world. Second, I will explore the initiatory practice of settling the *orixá* in a material object, which intimates a process of ontological hybridization between objects, bodies, and *orixás*, providing a framework for understanding religious affordances and the abilities required to engage with sacred or profane elements in religious practices. Finally, I will describe possession as the final step in the initiation process and examine how the simultaneous making of the person and the saint reveal Candomblé's theory of personhood and agency. *Making* entails carving pathways amidst a universe teeming with forces, directing energies toward distinct objectives, and establishing existential territories comprised of varied elements. Thus, Candomblé can be perceived as the art of making by modulating the *axé* that permeates different beings, whether they are metals, stones, people, or deities.

## 4.1 *Axé, Ferramentas,* and the Creative Process

Upon first encountering the universe of Candomblé, we are quickly drawn to its diverse array of objects, be they necklaces, musical instruments, clay artifacts, straw, or porcelain vessels. Each element intimates a relationship to a particular *orixá*, woven into a complex system organizing the cosmos. Amid the vibrant material culture of Afro-Brazilian religions, the objects that impressed on Nina Rodrigues the idea that its practitioners worshipped their deities by attributing supernatural powers to inanimate objects were the stones and iron tools in which the *orixás* "sit". The accusatory notion of fetishism, in which material things chosen at random would become the enchanted object of devotion of so-called primitive peoples – fetishes (from the Portuguese word *feitiço*, meaning charm or sorcery) – indicated a perceived mental confusion, where the distinction between the realms of immanence and transcendence, the material and the spiritual, was supposedly unclear (Latour, 1996/2010).

Working out the cognitive and ontological implications of sacred objects in Candomblé is an essential task for anyone looking to locate the meaning of the materialized ritual practices of this tradition. We will begin by looking at those objects that are forged, like the *ferramentas* (tools), and not just found, like the *otás* (stones). *Ferramentas*, from their production and transformation in the hands of artisans to their re-making in the ritual sitting or settling that accompanies the initiation of new *iaôs* are a window into not only how practitioners interact materially with their deities, but also how personhood is wrought from the displacement of *axé* that occurs in the way things and people are "made."

Lucas Marques (2023) provides us with a rich ethnography of tool-making drawn from his experiences shadowing José Adário dos Santos (b. 1947), better known as Zé Diabo (see Figure 3), perhaps the last great religious blacksmith forging *ferramentas* in Salvador, Bahia. Whereas each *orixá* reigns over a distinct array of material substances embodying their essence and facilitating their manifestation in the physical world, iron falls under the dominion of Ogum. Revered as the patron of agricultural wisdom and, notably, the divine artisan who commands metals, Ogum presides over warfare and technology, holding a significant position as the second deity in the Afro-Brazilian pantheon, closely intertwined with and surpassed only by Exu. All creative endeavors must flow through Ogum's domain, the lord of pathways, who possesses the power of unlocking them. Marques quotes Zé Diabo as asserting that "Ogum is everything. Everything has to have Ogum. Every tool carries Ogum, the [work] of Ogum. There is nothing you can do without him" (2023, 187).

Zé Diabo exclusively crafts tools for *orixás* associated with iron, especially Exu and Ogum (see Figure 4), but also Oxóssi, Obaluaiê, Ossanha, Tempo, and

**Figure 3** Zé Diabo welding agogôs in his workshop in Bahia (2013)
Photograph by Lucas Marques. Used with permission.

**Figure 4** Exus and Ogum in Zé Diabo's workshop in Bahia (2013)
Photograph by Lucas Marques. Used with permission.

Oxumarê – all of whom are either regarded as hunter or warrior deities. Evincing the notion that engaging with different materials would necessitate tapping into alternative energies and traversing distinct paths than those to which he was called, Zé Diabo states, "I was born to work the iron, in the rough. I was raised like that. It was Ogum who made me this way" (2023, 187). But although every piece of iron has the energy of Ogum, not all iron is created equal: "some irons are considered to be stronger or more alive than others. Rusted irons, for example, are more powerful, because they carry more energy (*axé*) of the *orixá*" (Marques, 2023, 188). If the iron being worked comes from artifacts associated with Ogum, including screws, anchors, nails, knives, swords, or chains – materials that are deemed raw and believed to concentrate the *axé* of the *orixá* – they will require less manipulation by the blacksmith. Marques fittingly concludes that the work of Zé Diabo in his workshop consists of 'channeling certain energies through the various transformations that irons go through – from the raw material to a *terreiro*' (2023, 189).

The process of crafting a tool is influenced by the *orixá*'s desires regarding the material object, ensuring it will serve as a suitable seat or settlement for the deity. This is exemplified in a narrative recounted by Marques, where Exu was alleged to have provided particular instructions to a woman who visited the workshop to consult with Zé Diabo. She entered the workshop carrying a small piece of paper containing sketches, notably featuring Exu holding a trident, one of the prevailing shapes used for making Exu's *ferramentas* and the reason why Zé Diabo (lit., Devil Joe) got his nickname.[23]

> She handed the paper to Zé Diabo, who promptly opened it and examined it at length. Dona Dalva then explained that she had dreamed of her Exu, and, as soon as she woke up, she had intuitively drawn it on a piece of paper. "It was Exu who requested," she said, "he wants to be made this way." Studying the paper, Zé Diabo asked her a few questions in order to discover the quality[24] of the deity and what the iron would "accept" from the sketch. He asked, for example, if the line on his head was a hat and if his head would have to be uncovered or not. In addition, he said that the key should be attached to Exu's foot by a chain because he is the only one who has the power to open and close doors. Finally, he said that the key and trident had to be made with a 3/8 iron;[25] otherwise, the tool would not last long. Dona Dalva agreed and said she would need the tool for the following week, as the deity was demanding to be made. Zé Diabo then settled a price for the order, and she gave him an advance. (Marques, 2023, 189)

Marques narrates that following discussion with his client, Zé Diabo transferred her sketches onto another piece of weathered paper, accentuating the hat, horns, key, and trident with new lines. With a measuring tape in hand, he envisioned the proportions of the *ferramenta*. However, despite serving as a reference for the forthcoming creation, the drawing did not offer a precise blueprint of the final object. Thus, Marques argues that rather than a conventional project, the drawing represented Zé Diabo's interaction with Dona Dalva's Exu, allowing him to perceive the *orixá*'s forms and proportions through a dynamic dialogue. This communication accounted for the desires of the *orixá* as well as the characteristics and potential transformations of the iron itself. As Marques quotes Zé Diabo as remarking, "everything has to have its size, its place in the world. If you have drawn something wrong, it is useless, the iron will not obey, it will not want to be made that way" (2023, 189).

Note that Dona Dalva and Zé Diabo are quoted as saying, respectively, that Exu demands *to be made* and that there is a specific way the iron wants *to be*

---

[23] Exu is often associated with the devil in popular perception (Marques, 2023, 190–191), reflecting and causing further prejudice against Afro-Brazilian religions. Mariano Carneiro da Cunha (1983) explains that depictions of Exu with horns, tridents, and tails stem from African influences rather than a direct link to the Christian devil in Christianity, while Jim Wafer (1991) suggests that the conflation of Exu with the devil underscores Exu's distortion through Christian perspectives on evil and the devil's reinterpretation within Candomblé.

[24] Here, quality (*qualidade*) represents a variation of an *orixá*. For instance, Ogum Xoroquê (from Yoruba, lit. the one who cuts fiercely) is considered one of Ogum's qualities, while Tranca Rua (lit., one who locks streets) is a quality attributed to Exu. A distant analogy can be drawn with the distinct aspects of Marian devotions, such as Our Lady of Navigators (syncretized with Iemanjá in southern Brazil) or Our Lady of the Immaculate Conception (syncretized with Oxum).

[25] A cylindrical and solid iron bar, approximately 0.56 kg/m and about 9.5 mm in diameter.

*made*. The Portuguese for this expression – *ser feito* – is the equivalent of *being initiated*, and this is no coincidence. As we will see, *feitura*, the act of making and a synonym for initiation in Afro-Brazilian religious jargon, involves an ontological dynamic that will result in the construction of the person as a relational complex. Finding or, in the case of iron-related *orixás*, making their material seat or settlement evinces the idea of channeling energies and refers to the fact that, in Candomblé, every entity pulsates with *axé*. Moreover, Bastide (1958/2010) proposed that all entities possess varying degrees of existence determined by the intensity of *axé* within them. For instance, a seemingly ordinary stone can serve as the seat of a deity, or hold remarkable energy due to its history and use in rituals, or simply carry the *axé* of an *orixá* as any ordinary stone would. Bastide emphasizes that this spectrum of existence is not just a matter of logical categorization but rather a continuum of participation, ranging from mere association to profound identification (Marques, 2018). Thus, between absolute being and non-being lies an infinite array of modulations that distinguish entities. Within this interconnected system, all entities – humans, tools, natural elements, *orixás* – are infused with the same sustaining "lines of force." Bastide calls this the *principle of participation*, inspired by Lucien Lévy-Bruhl's concept of *participation mystique* – a kind of attachment to objects in which subjects cannot clearly differentiate themselves from their respective objects. However, not all entities participate with each other indiscriminately; rather, such interactions occur within specific frameworks. For entities to engage with one another, they must exist within the same reality domain, adhering to a predetermined classification system of the cosmos. Building on Émile Durkheim's work, Bastide introduces the *principle of cutting*, which delineates various domains where participation occurs. Nonetheless, Bastide argues that these domains are interconnected through "analogies," or what he terms the *principle of correspondences*, influenced by Marcel Griaule. The fusion of these seemingly divergent principles – Lévy-Bruhl's participations, Durkheim's classifications, and Griaule's correspondences – constitutes the ontological foundation of what Bastide termed the subtle philosophy of Candomblé.

Drawing on Bastide's ideas, Goldman expands the notion of participation to propose a "basic monism" within Candomblé, where *axé* permeates everything in the universe through a process of differentiation and individuation (2007, 116). *Axé* exists in surplus within a "virtual" realm, actualized through ritual practice: each entity crystallizes or coalesces as a result of *axé*'s modulating flow, evolving from a general and homogeneous force into diversified and concrete manifestations. Goldman (2009) views *axé* as a pervasive force that traverses all aspects of existence in varied forms, and he sees it as offering an alternative perspective on the creative process. Rather than the conventional addition of elements, this process involves refining and actualizing preexisting potentialities, akin to the sculpting of raw material into form. Thus, as Marques aptly concludes, making, in Candomblé, should be thought of less as creation and more as a process of composition and individuation of a series of forces that already exist excessively in the world (2023, 196).

After leaving the workshop, the *orixá* tool proceeds to a *terreiro*, where it undergoes a transformational process alongside other elements, culminating in the creation of the seat or settlement that constitutes the material manifestation of the deity. Once fashioned, it integrates with the individual, extending their energetic and bodily connection to the complex relationship between the initiate and their *orixá*. This phenomenon, akin to Alfred Gell's (1998, ch. 7) concept of a "distributed person," will be revisited as we delve further into initiation. As we will see next, the seat or settlement requires continual nourishment through offerings, sacrifices, and rituals involving cleansing with herbs, palm oil, or honey, all contributing to the dynamic exchange that fortifies the bond between the future *iaô* and the *orixá* until they are finally made one complex entity.

## 4.2 *Assentamentos*, Ontological Hybrids, and Affordances

Daniel Miller (2005, 25) observes that the more importance is given to immateriality, the more precisely the specific material form used to express that immateriality is exploited. In Candomblé, these expressions manifest in the section of the shrines known *assentos* (seats) or *assentamentos* (settlements), whose names evince the fixation of the saint in a material object. Typically, the shrines, or *ibás*, feature a dais adorned with various pots and containers, made of materials such as clay and porcelain, or sometimes wood, each wrapped in cloth and concealed from public view. Within these pots lie the *fundamentos*, the foundational elements embodying the "saints" of the initiates. Settlements can take various forms, with stones or pebbles (*otás*, sometimes spelled *otãs*) and iron tools, like the ones wrought by Zé Diabo, being among the most common. Each *orixá* possesses specific *fundamentos*: for instance, the seats of Oxum and Iemanjá are adorned with shells and stones found in bodies of water, representing their association with freshwater and the sea, respectively; they will also reflect their associated colors (yellow or gold for Oxum, white or silver for Iemanjá). Similarly, the stones associated with Xangô are regarded as having been cast to the earth as thunderbolts, symbolizing his domain as the deity of thunder (Sansi-Roca, 2005, 142).

As Rabelo attests, 'The making of the *orixá* in the head is accompanied –
sometimes preceded – by the settling of the *orixá* in the *terreiro*' (2011, 23).
Many initiates attest that their induction into Candomblé was not their choice
but was rather compelled or imposed by *orixás*, caboclos, or other entities,
binding them to devotion through obligation rather than mere faith. These
entities are held to wield the power to bring physical, mental, and social
upheaval to those chosen for their devotion if their responsibilities are not
fulfilled. When troubled individuals seek guidance in a *terreiro*, the priestess'
first action is to consult the cowrie shells and, through this oracle, to reveal the
identity of the patient's *orixás* along with the root causes of their suffering.
To alleviate their distress, a *bori* can serve as an initial step toward potential
initiation, as previously discussed. Recognizing the head as a vessel of *axé*,
"feeding the head" becomes a means to close the body off from malevolent
forces.

The *bori* ritual signifies the establishment of an alliance with the *orixá*, as it is
through the head (*ori*) that the *orixás* establish their connection with their
devotee. As we saw in Section 3, during this ceremony, offerings are presented
to the individual's head and their *orixá de cabeça* (head *orixá*). Various foods
are arranged on the patient's head and the altar dedicated to the *orixá*. The
remnants of the ritual are placed on the *orixá*'s altar, where they undergo a
transformation into an *assentamento*, marking the saint's presence within the
vessel. Consequently, the patient becomes integrated into the collectivity of the
house as a novice and, even without full initiation, assumes obligations to both
the *orixá* and the community. Positioned within the hierarchical framework led
by the priestess, the patient is now obligated to participate in the regular ritual
washing of the seat. These altars are discreetly tucked away in the *orixá*'s
chambers, permanently fixed and accessible solely to the priestess.

The meaning of the settlements arises from the engagement that people
maintain with them, which exists and persists solely through this engagement,
so that they are not independent of their materiality or their sensible qualities,
but are rather interwoven through them, in the relationship between the bodies
of the adepts and their material, sensible, localized presence in the *terreiro*.
Moreover, Rabelo notes that the altars' hidden presence amplifies their potency,
which becomes tangible during possession rituals, an experience reserved only
for the initiated who can be possessed.

> In the chamber of the saints, a story is woven, invisible to outsiders, but quite
> clear and palpable to those in the house. A story of relationships between the
> adept and their saint, between them and their brothers- and sisters-of-saint,
> between everyone – gods and humans – and the mother- or father-of-saint of
> the house. The construction of this story is closely linked to the way in which

these sacred objects mobilize the body, soliciting care, demanding certain gestures and postures, inviting activity or passive contemplation. (Rabelo, 2011, 24)

When Rabelo discusses how objects mobilize, solicit, and even demand certain behaviors, she might just as well be saying that they *afford* such behaviors. A long phenomenological tradition which has influenced ecological psychology has recognized that humans perceive their environment as providing opportunities for action, not just receiving sense data but perceiving value-laden properties of things in the world. However, while James J. Gibson (1979, ch. 8) primarily spoke of affordances in the physical world, in religious rituals an agent perceives not only physical but also affective and social realities as offering opportunities for action. In other words, religious practices materially, affectively, and socially afford experiences in which participants develop the ability to respond to what they should and should not see, feel, and do – the full range of religiously shaped perceptions, emotions, and actions. This gives us a way to speak about *religious affordances* – solicitations of the abilities of an agent who must pay respect to the superempirical resources that make the practice successful and act according to the environment's sacred or profane features. Consequently, this perspective offers us a framework to understand religious practices not merely as mechanical rituals but as pathways to shaping one's identity, training individuals to perceive the world as offering opportunities for meaningful engagement and proper action.

If a philosophical framework for religious practices adopts this perspective, it will entail an examination of normative subjective experiences (Schilbrack, 2021). Given that ritual participants may not always articulate or even possess the ability to articulate these norms, as reflexivity and reasoned explanation are not prerequisites for participating in a religious form of life, the challenge in studying embodied religious experiences lies not in their privacy or inaccessibility, but rather in their tacit nature. To address this challenge, attention, phenomenological description, and critical reflection are essential to bring these experiences to the forefront of inquiry. Toward this end, Arnaud Halloy (2013) provides us with an impressive cognitive ethnography of the ontological dynamic of objects, bodies, and deities in Xangô, an Afro-Brazilian tradition that developed in the northeastern state of Pernambuco in similar ways to Candomblé. Halloy argues that initiation rituals involving "things" generate cognitively and emotionally salient *ontological hybrids*. That is because, crucially, the participants consider the introduction and manipulation of cultic objects more than a case of mere expression or representation. For the participants, as the saying goes, "the *otá* is the *orixá*." Moreover, practitioners habitually refer to the *otá* of their altar by the expression "my *orixá*" and that of other initiates as, for instance, "Maria's Oxum," "my brother's Ogum," and so forth.[26]

Roger Sansi-Roca (2005) emphasizes that the significance of finding the *otá* marks a foundational event in the relationship between the *orixá* and their human child, recognizing the active role played by the stone in this unique event. He labels this agency displacement "driven chance," as the *orixás* actively seek to be found and reveal themselves through the *otás*. The physical aspect of the stones, the ecological and mental circumstances surrounding their discovery, and the oracular procedure for their identification all contribute to their evocative potential (Halloy, 2013, 146). Furthermore, because practitioners equate *otás* (and *ferramentas*) with the *orixás* themselves, their influence over initiates is profound. For instance, Halloy (2013, 137) recounts a dramatic episode where, while cleaning up the remnants of an offering (*ebó*) at an altar, he accidentally discarded the small *otá* of an initiate's Iemanjá, despite a warning from the priest who had half-jokingly advised him not to throw out the *otá* with the *ebó*. As an initiate later explained to him, and as he personally experienced, losing the *otá* of an initiate constitutes a real spiritual drama. Numerous stories underscore the dire consequences of abandoning, mistreating, or outright destroying settlements and altars, including mutilation, burns, illness (both physical and mental), unfortunate encounters with authorities, and even sudden death.

Halloy describes the process connecting objects, bodies, and *orixás* in settlement and initiation as objects transforming into *object-gods* and object-gods becoming *object-bodies*. This radical shift in perception is brought about by what he terms "invert isomorphism," where living beings are treated as tools and artifacts are treated as living beings (Halloy, 2013, 149; cf. Liénard, 2006). During the sacrificial ceremony that typically follows the ritual washing of the medium during initiation with a special decoction of freshly picked herbs, the sacrificial blood is poured onto the *otá* or *ferramenta* comprising the altar before being poured onto the head and shoulders of the initiate, who kneels facing the altar of their *orixá*. Participants handle the objects with the utmost care, not because they are fragile, but because they are imbued with a new divine nature, transforming their status from passive to potentially active. In contrast, sacrificial animals are handled as mere artifacts, seen only in their physical form: their blood serves as the primary carrier of *axé*, and their organs are the main ingredients in offerings to *orixás*. Remarkably, a similar process occurs with

---

[26] It is within this individualized existence that *orixás* are often referred to as "saints," and it is in this individuated sense that they both sit or settle in material objects and possess initiates.

the initiate: it is as if the initiate is reduced to pure corporeality during ritual activity, and even more radically during possession.

Initiates who witness the systematic association of various objects and substances with the manipulation of their head and body – and experience their treatment responding to similar gestures and attitudes – are inclined to perceive these objects as their "external organs" (Sansi-Roca, 2005, 144), or more broadly, as their person "distributed" in the material environment (Gell, 1998). The frequent correlation between object/body manipulations and possession trance further deepens the intimate connection between the *otá* or *ferramenta*, the *orixá*, and the initiate's body, blurring the ontological boundaries between these three categories of entities.

The fact that stones or pieces of iron do not offer the same opportunities for action to those who are not acquainted with (or do not abide by) their meanings in Afro-Brazilian religious rituals suggests a distinction between an object's sensorimotor availability – or "natural" affordances – and those learned through shared expectations, constraining their use – its "cultural" affordances (Ramstead *et al.*, 2016). In the case of cultic objects, unlike the everyday use of stones and pieces of iron, *otás* and *ferramentas* are treated with heightened levels of attention and sensitivity (for instance, they are not used as tools or weapons). The "hijacking" of natural affordances is a specific feature of many cultic objects, which is why another anthropologist, Pierre Liénard, introduces the notion of "derived" affordances, which he defines as a new potential for action obtained by ritualizing ordinary behavior (Liénard, 2003, 295). While attempting to identify the cognitive processes at work in the ritual manipulation of objects among the Turkana people of northwest Kenya, Liénard argues that ritual action activates specific assumptions about the difference between living things and artifacts. Participants use living kinds as tools which thus acquire a function – an essential feature of our understanding of artifacts. Moreover, in sacrifice rituals, the Turkana manipulate artifacts as if endowed with a powerful inherent quality, or essence, a central feature of our understanding of living kinds (Liénard, 2006, 343-4), in a striking parallel with the manipulation of "object-gods" in Afro-Brazilian religions which go through a similar ontological hybridization, becoming "object-bodies."

The concept of cultural or derived affordances highlights a human propensity to assimilate cultural scripts without explicit instruction. In other words, it makes it possible to think about the implicit dimension of cultural learning at the crossroads of perception and action. This model forms the basis of a theory of cultural learning, which makes it possible to account for this implicit learning, namely a theory based on the articulation between attention regimes – ways of paying attention to things and people – and shared expectations following immersion in a given cultural practice or environment. In this model, representations are no longer at the heart of human cultures but rather forms of education of attention (Ingold, 2001) and skilled intentionality (Ramstead *et al.*, 2016): ways of connecting attentionally and responding to the demands of a material and social environment.

The learning process within Candomblé is gradual and meticulous, demanding both patience and dedication. As Goldman elaborates, it is an intricate journey that entails the accumulation of small fragments of knowledge over time.

> Novices in Candomblé are fully aware from the outset that there is no point in waiting to receive ready-made teachings from a master. Instead, they must patiently put together details gleaned here and there over the years, in hope that, at some point, this accumulation of knowledge will acquire enough density to be useful. This is called "gathering leaves," an expression related to the fact that knowledge and learning is located under the sign of the *orixás* [Ossanha], the master of herbs, and [Oxóssi], the hunter. Learning is then conceived above all as a form of search and capture, a pursuit that inevitably involves a certain degree of risk. (Goldman, 2007, 109)

Learning in Candomblé thus transcends mere accumulation of data or information, requiring the assimilation of knowledge to the core of one's being (Cossard, 1970, 227). This integration occurs gradually over time, through a slow-developing habit. This habit entails the immersion in rituals, gestures, words, dances, and melodies, eventually forming inseparable automatisms. As we will see in Section 5, such integration emerges through active participation in contextual practices and bodily and affective engagement with both the environment and its inhabitants. Crucially, this process involves a profound correspondence: as the bonds between the individual and the *orixá* are forged and nurtured, the *orixá* within the individual also evolves throughout the journey.

## 4.3 Making the Person, Making the Saint

Although the settlement serves as the saint's enduring and concealed presence, it is the dancing body of the devotee that truly embodies the *orixá*, even if its presence is fleeting. As Sansi-Roca (2005) observes, while in the seat the saint is nourished, during celebrations, the incorporated saint takes on the role of the host; while the seat conceals the saint, within the body of the initiate, the saint emerges publicly and triumphantly; while in the seat the saint remains fixed, in the human body the saint dances. Possession is thus the third, final, and pivotal ingredient in initiation in this cluster of traditions in which individuals are not inherently formed but are shaped through a protracted process.

In Candomblé, initiation, *feitura* (lit., making) or "making the saint" (*fazer o santo*) encompasses the process of constructing the person in relation to the entities that they incorporate as well as the "other body" of these spirits, the altars. Augras (1986), Segato (2005), Goldman (2007), and others converge on the idea that *feitura* connotes that the *orixá* is recreated or "made" in a specific human body as an individual *orixá* (the "saint") while the initiates themselves are "made" because "a person is not born readymade but constructed during the long process of initiation" (Goldman, 2007, 111–112). This underscores how the initial possession not only molds the initiate but also imbues the *orixá* with identity, since, initially, the *orixá* lacks distinctiveness, existing as a generic entity.

As we have seen, the creation of an individual *orixá* begins in the settlement process. When the saint is seated on the head of the new child and settled on a stone or iron tool, from that moment on and throughout life, there will be a specific and unique object that will literally be the person's saint, as we have seen. As Rita Laura Segato observes, the language used to refer to settlements emphasizes the fundamental notion that, although each individual belongs to an *orixá*, they only embody a personal and unrepeatable instance of that *orixá*.

> Thus, there are as many saints as there are people and, using the *orixá* Xangô here merely as an example, although many individuals are children of Xangô, in no case do two of them possess the same Xangô, not even if they share the same quality of that god. Therefore, two children of Xangô Aganju[27] will still be two different Xangôs when possessed, and will have two different stones, each one being the particular Xangô seated for each of these children. Furthermore, if a mother or father-of-saint has five children of Xangô, they will keep in their holy room five different stones set as Xangôs, one for each of them. (Segato, 2005, 96)

The same point about unrepeatability, of course, goes for the settling of the *orixá* in the head and, consequently, for possession. Through the act of possession, the *orixá* transitions into an individual entity, acquiring gendered attributes and a distinct personality. This transformative process is pivotal, leading to the realization that 'a more or less undifferentiated individual ... becomes a structured person and a generic *orixá* ... is actualized as an individual *orixá*' (Goldman, 2007, 112). This is why *orixás* are perceived both as natural forces and as distinct spiritual beings: these manifestations refer to different expressions of the *orixá*, namely, the generic, force-of-nature expression, and the

---

[27] In Cuba and other countries of the Afro-Atlantic diaspora, Aganju is venerated as a distinct *orixá*. In Candomblé, however, Aganju is a quality that embodies the aspect of Xangô associated with explosiveness and lack of control, symbolizing the personification of volcanoes.

individual, personal-saint expression. This gives us a way to distinguish between the *orixás* whose narratives are recounted in the myths and those capable of manifesting within a human form and settling in material objects.

An important goal of initiation is taming the body, preparing it to receive the saint (Sansi, 2009, 144). Initially, due to its lack of regulation, the *orixá*'s manifestation in possession can be intense, forceful, and uncontrolled. Indeed, before initiation it is not uncommon for people to be possessed haphazardly. However, through the long process of initiation, the individual learns to incorporate and manage the presence of the *orixá* within their body. Following an extended period of seclusion to learn the secrets of the tradition deemed appropriate to transmit to a novice – such as songs, the use of leaves, and sacrificial rites – the initiate emerges for the priestess to shave the new *iaô*'s head, mixing the blood with *axé*-rich elements and adorning it with the motifs of the initiate's head *orixá*. Finally, the initiate comes out for the public ritual known as *saída de iaô* (lit., *iaô*'s exit), signifying the completion of the initiation process through the inaugural possession.[28]

*Feitura* thus goes beyond mere education in myths, songs, and prayers, although it does encompass those elements. From the sacrificial offerings to feed the initiate-in-training's head in *bori*, through the sitting of the saint on the head and settling the saint on a stone or iron tool, and finally in the initial incorporation of the *orixá*, initiation at once makes the saint and the person. Through this complex process, the *orixá* becomes more than just a generic entity, now embodying the unique characteristics of the individual. The *orixá* becomes personalized. At the same time, initiation lays the groundwork for the development of the initiate's identity, shaped over time through mutual interaction with the saint. After seven years, the initiate may receive authorization to establish their own *terreiro*, granting them the authority to initiate (or "shave") others. However, the new house's *axé* will always maintain a connection to the original house, ensuring the continuity of lineage and tradition.

The relationship between the initiate and their saint is not always smooth, however. As Augras relays, in the *terreiros* she studied in Rio de Janeiro, "certain *orixás* are experienced by their children in the mode of absolute alterity, imposed in spite of the will of the children" (Augras, 1986, 195). Furthermore, individuals frequently assert that possession occurs at the will of the deity to descend, rather than stemming from the initiate. Attempting to explore this matter further or understand the nuanced boundary between what is considered a "normal" state of consciousness and the state of possession is often regarded

---

[28] This sequence of events represents the ideal scenario in initiation rites. However, the process may sometimes unfold in less controlled or structured ways (cf. Segato, 2005, 102).

as intrusive or disrespectful. Such inquiries violate the privacy entitled to those who undergo such manifestations and discussing the behaviors or utterances of individuals during possession may provoke embarrassment or even feelings of shame for them. Segato uses this kind of tension to talk about *feitura* as a process of accepting another within oneself which includes the negotiated relationship between the self and the saint. This begs a point about agency:

> It is common for people to refuse responsibility for the saint's exuberant deeds or ways of expressing themselves during possession. Whether on the part of the protagonists themselves or those assisting the possession, the language used to refer to the phenomenon is intended to emphasize the disconnection or estrangement between a possessed person and the *orixá* that "descended" on them (I've never come across any confusing statements regarding who said or did something: an individual or their *orixá*). A very common example of the way in which the *orixás* apparently act in blatant contradiction to the wishes of their children is by making them, while possessed, hug people with whom they have quarreled. This is, among other things, an indicator of the boundary that separates the self from the saint. (Segato, 2005, 100)

In *The Fetish Revisited*, J. Lorand Matory recognizes that "Spirit possession is the most dramatic public demonstration of the vessel-based Yorùbá-Atlantic model of the person" (2018, 11). This "vessel self" (2018, 290) is characterized by the copresence of opposite beings and its elements reflect contingent historical processes of encounter in the trans-Atlantic zone. Matory further proposes that the Afro-Atlantic self is compound, fractal, networked, and a "crossroads of forces" (2018, 286). However, in his review of Matory's book, Steven Engler (2019) points out that while Matory is avowedly inspired by Bruno Latour's (1987) networked notion of the self and draws from Gell's (1998) idea of a fractal self formed in relation to objects, he nevertheless rejects the extended view of agency which is its counterpart. Matory acknowledges that this reflects his own trajectory of "Western self making" (2018, 184):

> I affirm that things do participate in a collectively and historically human-made world that … [affects] people as powerfully as I am affected by a red traffic light … .. However, partly because I am a child of the West, I also resist Latour's wish to attribute such a degree of agency to things. I cannot resist my doubts that things intend, dictate, or act. … I am uncomfortable with the degree to which these models shift agency and even volition away from human beings. (Matory, 2018, 185–186)

As in the case of recognizing the agency of objects, recognizing the agency of incorporated spirits involves an altered conception of agency. Contrary to the zero-sum assumption that granting agency to objects or other-than-human persons diminishes it for humans, Candomblé challenges conventional Western notions of agency by redistributing it among individuals and objects in a more fluid and contingent manner. Departing from the notion of the self as the sole locus of control and meaning attribution, it affirms the agency of both humans and non-human entities. Just as acknowledging the agency of objects like *ferramentas* and *otás* requires reevaluation, understanding the agency of incorporated spirits entails a broader reimagining rather than a simple relocation of agency. As Goldman (2012) suggests, Candomblé blurs the line between the "made" and the "given" by engaging human agency in ongoing dialogue with spirits, deities, and objects. This reciprocal relationship between human and non-human agents has the potential not only to deepen conceptions of agency but also to transform our own capacity for agency as theorists, prompting us to approach subjects without preconceptions and to dynamically explore the multifaceted nature of agency.

## 5 A Religion of Embodied Knowledge

"Candomblé is a religion 'of the hand'," Paul Christopher Johnson states, borrowing from a priestess, "performed in a factory, where there is little attention devoted to abstract theologizing" (2002, 49). Perhaps even more aptly, Motta (2005) and others describe it as a religion of the *body* – that is, of the whole body. As Ana Paula Silveira explains in her ethnography of Batuque, an Afro-Brazilian tradition that developed in the southern state of Rio Grande do Sul in similar ways to Candomblé:

> In Afro-Brazilian religions in general, the body is perceived as a whole and must be activated in order to learn to take care of oneself and to value the experiences made in the world, to learn to be-in-the-world now. The initiation process recovers a natural and social identity that has been lost for various reasons, but which has been present since birth. This is the memory of the body, which is ritually reactivated and fixed through long stages of learning and incorporating the fundamentals of religious life through dance and music. (Silveira, 2008, 109)

However, it is not only that the body figures centrally in Afro-Brazilian religious practice as its main instrument of ritual devotion. As Seligman observes, "experiencing and even inviting changes to one's bodily state is an essential element of this practice" (2014, 19). Furthermore, the body is not only the source and instrument for the movements of ritual prostration, dancing, and spirit possession, as well as the consumption of ritual foods, and the accumulation and transfer of *axé*. The body, in Afro-Brazilian religions, is the source and instrument of learning, understanding, and knowledge.

In this final section, I will defend the adoption of an embodiment paradigm in the philosophy of religion by showing that it is needed to make sense of religious practices as cognitive enterprises. I will draw on to argue that perceiving dance as a vehicle for embodied knowledge can lead to an enriched epistemological framework that appreciates how religious as well as nonreligious understanding can be nurtured through bodily experience. I will then explore a related form of embodied knowledge by exploring affective learning processes through somatic signatures in the context of spirit possession. Finally, I will conclude with a reflection on the need for a religious epistemology that better acknowledges the sense-making capacities and affective responses of embodied human beings in a material sense.

## 5.1 An Embodiment Paradigm

After diagnosing traditional philosophy of religion, Schilbrack contends that we should adopt an embodiment paradigm to see religious practices as thoughtful (2014, xiv). Such a paradigm would entail conceiving a religious body not only as a passive object on which culture operates but also as the seat of subjectivity and religious being-in-the-world, helping us understand how embodied, situated, and materially extended practices are properly cognitive. Schilbrack recognizes that the philosophical study of religious practices is a relatively unexplored field. The traditional division of labor in religious studies ascribes the study of religious beliefs to philosophy as if the mind was its proper object of concern. In contrast, it ascribes the study of the practical, material, and social aspects of religious phenomena to the social sciences: anthropology, sociology, psychology, and history. However, this division of labor does not do justice to the philosophical tools developed in the last decades (Porcher and Carlucci, 2023).

The body became a significant source of philosophical attention in the phenomenological tradition. In *Phenomenology of Perception*, Maurice Merleau-Ponty (1945) conceives the body as a non-dualistic, active, basic source of our relatedness to the world. He criticizes the then-prevailing Cartesian dualism for conceiving the soul and the body as two separate entities: the soul as immaterial, rational, and spontaneously active, and the body as a passive entity in a perceptual relation to the system of material objects. Schilbrack levels the same kind of criticism at the division of labor in the traditional philosophy of religion. It no longer needs to restrict itself to beliefs and doctrines, having theology and sacred texts as its only source, since it can now investigate the body as an actor in religious practices.

The anthropologist Thomas Csordas (1990) was responsible for bringing an embodiment paradigm to bear on religious studies. For Csordas, embodied cognition is more than a thesis that enables a new analysis of knowledge: it consists of a methodological perspective that takes the body as a condition for subjectivity and intersubjectivity, not a passive object determined by forms of social consciousness. That opens new paths to introduce different objects of study and renewed perspectives on religious practices, such as the role of the body in rituals. Nevertheless, despite a slow methodological shift in recent decades, the academic study of rituals still predominantly occupies itself with the study of symbols and abstract meanings referred to through semiotic analysis. Yet we cannot fully understand these practices with these methods alone. The way bodies interact during rituals and the actions of agents involved in them elicit the reactions of others. Again, the body is not simply a passive object on which cultures write their different meanings but is also the source of one's engagement with the world. Therefore, an embodiment paradigm is not only instrumental but essential to understanding the body's active role in rituals.

Various distinct cognitive mechanisms are engaged in various combinations in the diverse interactions we call rituals (Boyer and Liénard, 2020). By adopting an embodiment paradigm, we can begin to criticize those approaches to studying religious practices that assume they are thoughtless, non-cognitive enterprises. As Schilbrack observes, religious practices are not only expressions of religious thought but also instances of that thought. They are opportunities for cognition and inquiry about health, love, duty, maturity, sovereignty, purpose, or, more abstractly, the nature of human existence and the entities incorporated and honored (Schilbrack, 2014, 44). In participating in embodied religious practices, one learns about oneself, those with whom one interacts, the world, and the superempirical resources that make the practice successful (Schilbrack, 2014, 45). In other words, an embodiment paradigm allows us to recognize that the religious subject is an active inquirer and to see the body as the means through which practitioners investigate and create meaning.

In Afro-Brazilian religions, the absence of a unified, codified doctrine means that indoctrination occurs not through a shared text but through shared practices. Individuals learn and absorb the teachings through direct experience, transmitting actions and behaviors from one person to another. As we have seen, various embodied acts of devotion such as sacrifice, the intake of sacred foods, feasting, cleansing rituals, prostration, dancing, and the pivotal states of trance and possession, all are purported to increase levels of *axé*. Learning these practices serves as the primary means through which the more discursive elements are conveyed, as beliefs within Candomblé are seldom explicitly stated. In a similarly way to *axé*, knowledge about the spiritual world is gradually accumulated and internalized by participants through their active, embodied participation (Seligman, 2014, 36).

Through initiation and subsequent practice, worshippers acquire the skill to enter a trance state at appropriate moments during ritual performances triggered by induction cues such as specific drumming, singing, and dancing. By embodying spirits and deities, initiates establish a unique connection between themselves and those they become vessels for, allowing them to comprehend and experience the qualities of these entities as their own in a process that includes the learning of appropriate emotions.

## 5.2 Dance, Gestural Language, and Deutero-Learning

In contrast to the spirits of other Afro-Brazilian traditions, such as Umbanda, whose primary mode of communication is through speech, the *orixás* of Candomblé and parallel traditions, such as Xangô and Batuque, predominantly express themselves through intricate dance movements (see Figure 5). In fact, the primary way to identify a saint who has descended is by observing the distinct body movements of the possessed individual. As the saying goes, "the saint is known by their steps" (Segato, 2005, 102). These movements are believed to embody the personality of the saint, although this manifestation may not occur immediately upon possession, and it is often necessary to instruct the possessed individual on the proper dance movements that express the saint's identity. In her examination of what she terms the gestural language of Candomblé, Marlene de Oliveira Cunha (1986) expounds on some of these movements:

> For example, for Oxóssi, there is the gesture made with the hands that resembles a bow and arrow, a hunting instrument; for Iansã, the gesture of holding up the skirt, causing the wind to blow to scare away the "eguns", i.e. the dead; for Ogum, the gesture of thrusting out the chest that resembles a physical combat; for Xangô, the majestic gesture of raising his arms to greet those present; for Obaluaê, the curved posture, showing his closeness to the ancestors; for Oxum, the gestures of caring for the body, exalting her beauty and vanity; for Iemanjá, the gesture of rocking, which represents the figure of the mother (Cunha, 1986, 79–80)

Novice practitioners primarily learn about the characteristics of their saint through the process of initiation which enables them not only to understand these characteristics but also to experience and embody them as part of their own identity. In Afro-Brazilian religions, belief and practice are thus deeply intertwined, with the process of embodied learning serving as a crucial junction for religious formation. This means that the process of learning and practicing the intricate dance movements is not only a way of communicating with the *orixás* but also a way of becoming closer to them and internalizing their

**Figure 5** Incorporated mediums dancing in a *terreiro* in Bahia (2022)
Photograph by the author.

characteristics. Through this process, practitioners not only learn about the *orixás* but also create a deep and meaningful relationship with them.

Cunha (1986, 144) interprets several significant ritual movements as symbolizing connection to the earth, such as the rhythmic beating of the earth with the feet during dance and the ceremonial gesture of touching the earth, then the forehead and the back of the neck, as a form of salutation to both the sacred ritual space and the individual spirits (see Figure 6). Thus, ritual performance entails a structured movement vocabulary where specific gestures and movement sequences synchronize with particular rhythms – what Ângelo Cardoso (2006) calls the *language of drums* – each imbued with distinct cultural or religious significance. Yvonne Daniel maintains that while certain gestures and movement sequences may directly convey literal meanings, "the social circumstances of performers have created a deep reliance on the abstracted expressiveness of the dancing body and on nonverbal communication procedures" (2005, 63). The depth and intensity of a performance frequently emerge from

**Figure 6** Ogum in a *terreiro* in São Paulo (2010)
Photograph by Bettina Schmidt. Used with permission.

the visual projection of meaning through the breath accompanying specific movements or through newly explored dynamics within repetitive actions. Moreover, meaning resonates through visceral reactions to the kinesthetic and musical impact, embodying abstract realizations and knowledge.

As worshipers perform, they sense and learn. And as they continue to perform over time, in the process of music-making and dance performance, embodied knowledge is constantly consulted. It is a dynamic, practical referencing that can mean different things within a lifetime. Some ritual performers are only concerned with the musical and dance product that yields transformation. Others are interested in what the transformation means, the related embodied knowledge that usually has to do with healing the self and the community, balancing relationships between the cosmos and the ritual community. (Daniel, 2005, 66)

Miriam Rabelo and Rita Santos (2011) liken the Afro-Brazilian religious learning process to what Tim Ingold (2001) describes as the "education of attention." Ingold proposes rethinking knowledge acquisition not as a blend of innate capabilities and learned skills (enculturation or acquisition), but rather as a development of skills (or "enskilment") that involves directing and refining perceptions and actions within an environment. According to Ingold, the education of attention does not consist of transmitting information or instilling propositional knowledge into the minds of novices. Instead, it involves guiding novices in a rediscovery process, navigating a world of practices where they can experiment and hone their skills through a mix of improvisation and imitation (Ingold, 2001, 140). By emphasizing learning as an experiential and adaptive process, this approach accounts well for the development of practical and nuanced abilities within the cultural context of Candomblé. However, a caveat must be added: *showing* will often be done in a very indirect and roundabout way. Echoing Rabelo (2015), Marques notes that one of the first things a person learns when they come into contact with the world of Candomblé is that, in it, 'one cannot want to know everything, see everything, ask questions or listen too much. More than a simple rule of etiquette, such restrictions indicate this vital game of visibilities and invisibilities in accessing knowledge' (2022, 128). Gisèle Cossard reports from her experience as an *ialorixá* on the nuances of this game:

> It is up to the young [*iaô*] to learn everything that concerns the ritual and the *orixá*: how to take care of their sacred room, how to behave during Candomblé, and the different ceremonies. Gradually, they try to discover the secrets of Candomblé, the "foundation". In this sense, they will experience great difficulties, as no one will teach them the proper songs, dances, or gestures. Since you can't ask any questions, you should watch, with your head and eyes downcast, never showing that you're looking overly attentive or interested. They soon discover that too much curiosity can harm them. This is due, on the one hand, to the fact that the older ones do not seek to reveal what they know, as they run the risk of being overtaken by the younger ones, and on the other hand, because it is not good to learn too quickly, for as with everything in Candomblé, it can have extremely harmful consequences for you and for others in the event of a mistake. (Cossard, 1981, 139–140)

Thus, Afro-Brazilian religious learning is not depicted as a neatly structured and singular corpus of regulations and insights, akin to a codified doctrine enforced from above. Because of this, Goldman (2007) affirms that to engage in this learning process, one must acquire the ability to learn how to learn –

what Gregory Bateson (1972, 166–176) terms *deutero-learning*. This entails absorbing information and developing the capacity to critically contextualize it, understanding the conditions under which learning can take place. To do so, it is necessary to cultivate specific skills, such as the feigned listlessness to which Cossard alludes and that Rabelo (2015) terms "a sidelong glance," a discreet and quick look that seeks to see what is not directly visible to the novice's gaze. In short, learning involves exercising discretion, knowing how to balance the desire to learn with the respect for the secret and unknown, with a contrived indifference to the action taking place. This is why Marques (2022), speaking from his experience in Zé Diabo's workshop, argues that in Afro-Brazilian religious contexts we may also think of an "education of distraction."

## 5.3 Somatic Signatures and Affective Affordances

According to the influential framework developed by Paul Griffiths and Andrea Scarantino (2008), affects manifest as signs within actions, shaping and being shaped by reciprocal interactions in social settings. They are culturally scaffolded, both synchronously by objects and diachronically by social norms, challenging individualist theories that restrict affects to intracranial confines and overlook the influence of social contexts and objects on affective experiences. This gives us a framework for articulating how we perceive *affective affordances*, which manifest as elements of the environment associated with agents' emotions, guiding our focus toward particular objects to discern their emotional significance (Hufendiek, 2016). These objects serve as scaffolds for affective experiences, offering support for the emergence and modulation of affects based on the individual's affective structure, goals, and situational constraints.

In the prototypical scenario of cultural learning, characterized as triadic, the learner and expert coordinate actions in a shared environment, with the learner sensitized to the objects and affective reactions of the expert (Tomasello, 2006). Over time, objects within the environment acquire affective relevance, becoming part of the learner's repertoire of affordances. This implicit knowledge of objects' affective value is mobilized in interactive contexts, shaping the learner's engagement with the affective *niche* – a habitat that reflects and organizes our affective life, shaping our emotional experiences and interactions with the world (Krueger and Colombetti, 2018) – and allowing for interventions in the environment to regulate specific affects.

Halloy (2021) delineates two interconnected rationales for the relevance of affective affordances in elucidating episodes of spirit possession. Firstly, they play a pivotal role in explaining the capacity to internalize cultural scripts without explicit instruction, instead adapting individuals to the exigencies of their circumstances. Secondly, they serve as the foundation for cultural learning, fostering shared attention and intentionality among agents to attune them to the demands of their social and material environment. Since different niches facilitate different affordances shaped by coordinated actions, participating in possession rituals hinges on an immersive and embodied experience within a tradition's affective niche. While formal instruction offers some insight into the tradition, we have seen that it represents only a fraction of the initiate's education. True understanding arises from active involvement in the niche, where implicit and practical knowledge is gleaned, enabling the individual to grasp the nuances of the situation. Through repeated exposure and engagement, the initiate learns to discern relevant aspects of the ritual, to respond appropriately to stimuli, and to refine their perceptual, proprioceptive, and inferential faculties. This learning process culminates in a greater sensitivity toward the wide range of emotional cues found in the various activities associated with possession, including dancing, drumming, and singing.

In Xangô, Batuque, and parallel traditions, possession episodes unfold in three stages: (i) irradiation or approximation, (ii) manifestation, and (iii) *axêro*. Various emotions and sensations characterize each of these stages. The irradiation or approximation of the *orixá* is marked by a sensory overload, leading to somatic changes such as shivers, tremors, loss of balance, and sweating, among others. Despite this sensory overload, Halloy (2012, 190) notes a sense of invisibility prevailing throughout this phase. This invisibility refers to an amalgamation of stimuli that activate various sensory channels simultaneously, including auditory, olfactory, and visual stimuli. The initiate struggles to discern the origin of each stimulus, prompting a shift in focus from the external world to the self. This internalization process is crucial for possession, as the initiate must remain attuned to their own somatic sensations, indicative of the *orixá*'s presence. By maintaining focus on themselves, the initiates can discern what Halloy terms the *somatic signature* of their *orixá*. Segato reports:

> Most people say that their discomfort is very strong in the moments immediately before the manifestation and that they feel the urge to run away from what follows. However, in most cases, the group's conditioning and pressure to stay and become possessed are stronger than this impulse. These last moments, it is said, have different characteristics according to the saint, such as, typically: feeling intensely cold for Oxum, feeling intensely hot for Iansã, feeling dizzy for Iemanjá, or experiencing an abrupt and unpredictable loss of consciousness for Xangô. (Segato, 2005, 104)

Everyone who spoke to Segato about this phenomenon mentioned that, under normal circumstances, intense emotions surface when they listen to the musical repertoire associated with their saints, particularly specific sequences of songs within that repertoire. For some individuals, this experience triggers bouts of crying, potentially leading to possession. Segato (2005, 105) also recounts an incident during a *toque*,[29] where an elderly and respected member of the community, seated in a corner of the *terreiro*, began crying as soon as his saint's repertoire started playing. After a few minutes, the house leader escorted him to the saint's room, where he remained until the repertoire concluded. Later explanations revealed that he had been irradiated by his saint, but due to his fragile health, attributed to a heart condition, he was persuaded to "take the saint off" (*tirar o santo*). Despite this, it was noted that his crying consistently preceded manifestation. The *toque* of his *orixá* thus afforded an affective reaction which not only preceded, but elicited possession.

During manifestation, interaction and affective regulation occur intra and interpersonally, involving four key poles: (i) the *orixá*, (ii) the possessed individual, (iii) the specialists, and (iv) the assembly. The *orixá*, an external entity with agency, manifests themselves within the possessed individual through incorporation. Halloy (2012, 191ff.) observes a regulation process primarily between the possessed individual and the incorporated *orixá*. Employing proprioceptive abilities, the possessed individual discerns the affective cues of the embodied entity and adjusts them as necessary – they can either enhance or diminish the intensity of the entity's affective flow. Simultaneously, interpersonal regulation takes place between the possessed individual and the specialists, who coordinate actions based on observations of the possessed individual's behavior. The specialists may influence the possessed individual's behavior to evoke specific affects or modulate their intensity according to the ritualistic context. Furthermore, these two levels of interaction are interconnected. As the possessed individual acts to regulate the affects of the possessing entity, they are attentive to the specialists' guidance throughout the ritual. Conversely, the specialists are attuned to the possessed individual's behavior to adjust internal reactions related to the *orixá* accordingly.

Finally, during *axêro*, the initiate reclaims command over their own body through their proprioceptive skills. As the possession episode draws to a close, initiates frequently report experiencing a dual sensation of well-being and

---

[29] *Toque* literally means "beat." In Afro-Brazilian religions, each *orixá* has their own *toque*, which affords different affective reactions in different practitioners. Cardoso (2006, 247) explains that the attribution of specific rhythms to particular *orixás* in Candomblé primarily pertains to instrumental music for dance. However, when these rhythms accompany chants, their exclusivity to a particular deity diminishes significantly. For instance, a *toque* such as the *aderé*, linked to Ogum, is also used for songs dedicated to Oxalá, and the *ijexá*, associated with Oxum, may accompany songs for various orixás. Thus, the focus shifts from the rhythm's association with a specific deity to the song itself as the expression of reverence.

emptiness, often expressed through bouts of crying or laughter. In short, through active engagement, initiates cultivate the sensitivities necessary to navigate the intricacies of the affective dynamics inherent in possession rituals. This heightened awareness enables them to discern, regulate, and respond to the pertinent affective cues. Without these acquired abilities, the voluntary engagement in possession becomes unattainable, as initiates would lack the means to either guide the *orixás'* reactions or surrender to their influence.

## 5.4 The Need for an Embodied Epistemology

The Afro-Brazilian religious learning process thus integrates gestures, dances, melodies, and words into a practitioner's automatic behaviors through gradual participation in practice contexts and active engagement with both the physical environment and its spiritual inhabitants (Marques, 2023, 128–129). The knowledge transmitted in these settings, be it the gestural language and somatic signature of a particular *orixá*, or the corpus of rules and etiquettes of a particular *terreiro*, is arrived at through bodily interaction with the environment. This begs the question of what if anything an epistemology rooted in the notions of propositional or factual knowledge has to offer in the search for a framework for an Afro-Brazilian religious epistemology.

Understandably, the predominant epistemological interest in traditional philosophy of religion has been justification. When first I began wondering how one might go about engaging philosophically with Afro-Brazilian religions, and still very much in the frame of mind of traditional philosophy of religion, I jotted down the following two questions: "How can possession be seen as evidence in favor of their view of what happens to us upon bodily death?" and "How can offerings and sacrifices be seen as evidence in favor of their view of the nature of spirits and deities?" (Porcher, 2021). Recently, Hans Van Eyghen (2023) has investigated, in a manner unprecedented in analytic epistemology of religion, the justification of what he terms "spirit-beliefs," that is, beliefs in the existence or nature of supernatural beings that are not gods. He examines a wide variety of religions such as West African traditions and their Afro-Atlantic offshoots, but also Tibetan Bön, Siberian as well as South Indian (Nayaka) animism, and new religious movements, drawing on phenomenal conservatism and its application to experiences of God which he extends to other kinds of religious experiences.

Phenomenal conservatism is an influential stance on the justificatory power of experiences, asserting that individuals are prima facie justified in believing that things are as they appear in the absence of counter-evidence. The prima facie condition acknowledges that justification can be undermined by "defeaters," usually classified into rebutting defeaters, which support the negation of a proposition, and undercutting defeaters, which cast doubt on the reliability of the belief's basis. This stance is the foundation of Richard Swinburne's (2004) argument that there is no epistemically relevant difference between religious and non-religious experiences. While acknowledging that many religious experiences differ from "ordinary" sense experiences by not being public, Swinburne contends that this does not negate their evidential value. Swinburne only denies taking an experience at face value if it was made under unreliable conditions, in circumstances where similar claims have proven false, if the object of experience was absent, or if the experience was not caused by the presumed object. Van Eyghen explores how phenomenal conservatism supports spirit-experiences and while acknowledging numerous and conflicting accounts of spirit-experiences, he argues that differences in spirit-experiences are not necessarily mutually conflicting, since variations may arise from spirits' alternating moods or temperaments. Finally, aligned with Linda Zagzebski's (2011) perspective on the authority of testifiers, he asserts that spirit-experiences reported by others should be granted justificatory force since there are no compelling reasons to view subjects reporting spirit-experiences as unreliable testifiers.

Tackling "perception-like" experiences of spirits, which occur with different sense modalities, mostly visual, auditory, and tactile, Van Eyghen sees them as situations where a subject perceives a sensation, thought, or awareness as caused by a spirit – what Swinburne calls "seemings," acknowledging the potential for a different cause. He further divides them based on their directness, illustrated by the following example (Van Eyghen, 2023, 70ff.). Suppose Anne believes a spirit visited her after experiencing a strong cold shiver upon entering a room, while Adam believes a spirit visited him after seeing a peculiar being moving in his garden at twilight. While both felt a spirit visited them, Adam seems to have stronger justification. Anne's is termed an indirect experience as she interpreted bodily sensations, while Adam's, involving a direct visual image, is labeled a direct experience. Van Eyghen considers both internalist and externalist theories of justification, but even accepting process reliabilism, the assessment of indirect spirit-experiences is largely negative. Although there are no strong defeaters for the claim that certain bodily sensations can be caused by spirits, the presence of numerous alternative explanations for these sensations weakens the case for believing that spirits are the cause. In contrast, direct experiences fare better. Under phenomenal conservatism, subjects with direct spirit-experiences can attain prima facie justification for spirit-beliefs. Additionally, subjects can derive justification for a spirit's attributes directly from these experiences. Identifying a spirit's identity may rely on background knowledge, but the issues encountered in indirect experiences, stemming from numerous alternative explanations, are less prevalent or absent in direct experiences.

Although both mediumship and possession occur concurrently in some traditions, mediumship-experiences and possession-experiences diverge primarily in the degree of control and personality retained by the medium. In mediumship, the spirit's role is relatively limited, often confined to delivering messages, while possession episodes often involve spirits taking complete control of the subject's personality and body. While possessing spirits also convey messages, this aspect is not the focal point of possession-experiences, as it is in mediumship. Unlike perception-like spirit-experiences, mediumship-experiences justify beliefs linked to a spirit's existence and visual attributes. While these experiences do not provide initial justification for the existence of a spirit for most believers, they offer supporting evidence, reinforcing beliefs applicable to both the subject and observers. Van Eyghen thus concludes that possession-experiences, akin to mediumship-experiences, unveil the nature of a spirit but can especially justify beliefs regarding the possessing entity's behavior. As possession-experiences are often not recalled by the possessed subject, their primary role lies in justifying beliefs for witnesses rather than the subject.

As well argued and thoughtful an examination into the justificatory power of possession experiences can be, however, such epistemological interests are completely alien to and out of step with the traditions it purports to examine. Such an interest pertains to purely intellectual or, as Daniel shrewdly calls it, disembodied knowledge: knowledge devoid of the integrated somatic, intuitive understanding, and spiritual wisdom that their combination engenders.

> From the period of enslavement through to the present, disembodied knowledge has dominated the Americas as a valued social paradigm ... The lay public, including ritual community members, students, and others, has been encouraged to think of scientific theoretical knowledge as superior to, rather than equal to, practical, experiential, or kinesthetic knowledge ... Institutions such as schools, churches, government, and the modern family have stressed the importance of specialization and compartmentalization. Certainly the performing and plastic arts (dance, music, sculpture, painting, architecture, and theater) are given importance in these institutions, but usually as subsidiary units of the "important" or "real" knowledge; that is, theoretical and scientific knowledge. (Daniel, 2005, 57)

In light of the preceding discussions regarding the practices and learning processes of Afro-Brazilian traditions, it should be apparent that the knowledge acquired and transmitted through these practices is *embodied knowledge*. In this context, Burley (2024) references the *Dictionary of Human Geography*'s fitting definition of embodied knowledge as "knowledge that is partial, situated, and developed through experience, contextualized with respect to the body, circumstances, life history, and locational context" (Castree, Kitchin, and Rogers, 2013, 125) as well as Rachel Elizabeth Harding's characterization: "A way of experiencing a relationship to history, to divinity, to ancestry from within the movements of one's own body" (2006, 17). Thus, Burley rightly notes that the concept of embodied knowledge, as explored by these authors and embodied in Afro-Brazilian religious practice, goes beyond Ryle's notion of "knowledge-how" – the ability to perform tasks, which Ryle contrasts with "knowledge-that" or factual knowledge (Ryle, 1945–1946, 4). In the context of Afro-Brazilian somatic and affective learning, embodied knowledge possesses a richer experiential dimension than mere enskilment. Accordingly, Burley describes it as a form of "knowledge by acquaintance," Bertrand Russell's term to describe direct awareness of an object (Russell, 1910–1911, 108), noting, however, that practitioners experience such acquaintance so intimately that it transforms their sensations and bodily comportment.

For instance, Elizabeth Pérez (2022) highlights that Afro-diasporic traditions exhibit what she refers to as "ethnosymptomatology" – the belief that the body's various parts are owned by specific beings, and they may utilize their "property" to convey messages. Sensations experienced in the gut are thus experienced not merely as bodily sensations but rather as signals of spiritual beings manifesting within it. Through somatic experiences and muscle memories, practitioners of Afro-diasporic traditions develop intimate relationships with their protecting deities, and gut feelings become the media for communication between these entities and human beings. As we have seen, the experience of *orixás'* somatic signatures plays a role in understanding religious cognition as embodied and extended beyond the confines of the head.

Pérez underlines the importance of including non-Euro-American models of "mind" along the gut–brain axis, evoking Diana Paton's observation that the concept of religion has been a race-making category, "a marker of the line between supposedly 'civilized' peoples (who practice religion) and 'primitive' peoples (who practice superstition or magic)" (Paton, 2009, 2), perpetuating the marginalization of African and Afro-diasporic traditions and reinforcing anti-Blackness. By broadening the category of "cognitive" to incorporate the whole body, we can recast Afro-diasporic religions as more than mere repositories of magic spells, acknowledging their profound intellectual contributions and recognizing Black Atlantic knowledges as such. Such an attitude offers us a similar benefit to realizing that differentiating between black (and/or Black) magic and religion lacks significant practical value. Instead, such distinctions have often been used to justify the marginalization of stigmatized and minority groups.

Thus, to forge ahead in the philosophical engagement with the traditions presented in this Element, we need to pursue a framework for an epistemology of religion that emphasizes the body's role in cognition. Only then will we be able to recognize religious practices not just as raw material for theory but as instances of religious thought, to challenge the notion that the brain is the sole locus of knowledge, and to decolonize disciplinary formations by defying the dominance of the head in the study of religion.

## Conclusion

> Allons! we must not stop here.
> Whitman, *Song of the Open Road*

I have offered Afro-Brazilian traditions as examples to highlight the limited reach of the philosophy of religion. This limitation exists not only because these traditions have been largely neglected, but also because the field lacks an appropriate framework for engaging with them. Again, this is because the philosophy of religion has focused on the doxastic aspects of text-based and institutionalized traditions while, for the most part, ignoring the practical and embodied aspects involved in liturgical performances. For this reason, it is necessarily at a loss regarding what to say about the central phenomena of traditions such as Candomblé, namely, spirit possession, dancing, singing, and the preparation, consumption, and offering of ritual foods. In this Element, I have sketched ways of engaging philosophically with such practices by drawing on mythic narratives and ethnographies as sources, employing resources from cultural anthropology, ecological psychology, and embodied cognitive science, and refraining from generalization and homogenization.

Schilbrack has recently voiced a concern about the potential pitfalls associated with diversifying the philosophy of religion. He worries that, in an attempt to show respect for diverse religious perspectives, philosophers may distance themselves from their distinctive role in the interdisciplinary field of religious studies: the evaluation of the truth of religious beliefs, the morality of religious practices, the veridicality of religious experiences, and the justice of religious institutions (2023, 308). I agree with Schilbrack that normative evaluation is that contribution to the study of religion which only philosophy can make. Moreover, I also agree with Sonia Sikka (2023) that studying worldviews such as those exemplified by Afro-Brazilian religions without engaging with them as dialogical partners in a philosophical conversation means they will continue to be excluded from reasoned debates about what is true, real, good and just. However, like Burley

(2012), I see evaluation as one among many tasks of philosophy and, at a moment when our grasp of certain religious forms of life is still tenuous, we should linger on contemplation and critical description (Phillips, 2001).

One cannot evaluate what one does not understand and there are several reasons why philosophers should be concerned about a lack of a good understanding of what certain religious practices mean. Such practices may be embedded in a culture that is geographically, temporally, or conceptually foreign to ours. The practices may evoke a visceral response, as in cases such as cannibalism, self-immolation, and animal sacrifice (Burley, 2020). Furthermore, if there is a history of oppression of those in the culture under study, which has been and, regretfully, still is the case for Afro-Brazilian religions, the philosopher's understanding will likely be shaped by structures of bias that need identification and correction before meaningful evaluation can occur. Contemporary philosophers of religion have not yet done conceptual justice to the variety of religious forms of life in the world and human history, and for each case where that is true, we are not at the point where we can move from critical description to evaluation. However, I am confident that through contemplating religious forms of life, we can progressively locate the meaning of beliefs and practices from an emic perspective while drawing on interdisciplinary resources in the study of religion.

# References

Agada, A and Attoe, AD (2023) Shifting perspectives in African philosophy of religion. Religious Studies 59, 291–293.

Akintoye, SA (2010) A History of the Yoruba People. Dakar: Amalion.

Amaral, R (2002) Xirê!: O Modo de Crer e de Viver no Candomblé. Rio de Janeiro: Pallas.

Aróstegui, NB (1994) Los orichas em Cuba, 2nd ed. La Habana: Unión.

Augras, M (1983/2008) O duplo e a metamorfose: A identidade mítica em comunidades Nagô. Petrópolis: Vozes.

Augras, M (1986) Transe e construção de identidade no Candomblé. Psicologia: Teoria e Pesquisa, 2(3), 191–200.

Awolalu, JQ and Dopamu, A (1979) West African Traditional Religion. Ibadan: Onibonoje Press.

Balogun, OA (2009) The nature of evil and human wickedness in traditional African thought: Further reflections on the philosophical problem of evil. Lumina 20, 1–20.

Banerjee, M (2021) Cultivating Democracy: Politics and Citizenship in Agrarian India. New York: Oxford University Press.

Bastide, R (1945) Imagens do Nordeste Místico em Branco e Preto. Rio de Janeiro: Cruzeiro.

Bastide, R (1958/2010) O Candomblé da Bahia: Rito Nagô. São Paulo: Companhia das Letras.

Bateson, G (1972) Steps to an Ecology of Mind. Chicago: The University of Chicago Press.

Beniste, J (2006) Mitos Yorubás: o outro lado do conhecimento. Rio de Janeiro: Bertrand Brasil.

Bergad, L (2007) The Comparative Histories of Slavery in Brazil, Cuba, and the United States. Cambridge: Cambridge University Press.

Bewaji, J (1998) Olodumare: God in Yoruba belief and the theistic problem of evil. African Studies Quarterly 2, 1–17.

Bishop, J (1998) Can there be alternative concepts of God? Noûs 32, 174–188.

Boyer, P and Liénard, P (2020) Ingredients of "rituals" and their cognitive underpinnings. Philosophical Transaction of the Royal Society B375, 20190439.

Burley, M (2012) Contemplating Religious Forms of Life: Wittgenstein and D. Z. Phillips. London: Bloomsbury.

Burley, M (2020) A Radical Pluralist Philosophy of Religion: Cross-Cultural, Multireligious, Interdisciplinary. London: Bloomsbury.

Burley, M (2022) African religions, mythic narratives, and conceptual enrichment in the philosophy of religion. Religious Studies 58, 1–17.

Burley, M (2023) Ethnographically informed philosophy of religion in a study of Assamese goddess worship. In Loewen, NRB and Rostalska, A (eds.), Diversifying Philosophy of Religion: Critiques, Methods, and Case Studies. London: Bloomsbury, pp. 177–193.

Burley, M (2024) "Not so much thought out as danced out": Expanding philosophy of religion in the light of Candomblé. Religious Studies, 1–13.

Burton, RF (1864) A Mission to Gelele, King of Dahome. London: Tinsley Brothers.

Cardoso, ANN (2006). A Linguagem dos Tambores. PhD dissertation, Universidade Federal da Bahia.

Carneiro da C M (1983) Arte Afro-Brasileira. In Zanini, W. (Org.). História geral da arte no Brasil, vol. 2. São Paulo: Instituto Walter Moreira Salles, pp. 1973–1033.

Carneiro, E (1948/2019) Candomblés da Bahia. São Paulo: Martins Fontes.

Castree, N, Kitchin, R, and Rogers, A (2013) A Dictionary of Human Geography. Oxford: Oxford University Press.

Cossard, G (1970) Contribution à l'Étude des Candomblés du Brésil: Le Rite Angola. PhD dissertation, École des Hautes Études en Science Sociales.

Cossard, G (1981) A Filha de Santo. In Moura, CEM (ed.), Olóòrisà: Escritos sobre a Religião dos Orixás. São Paulo: Ágora, pp. 129–151.

Courlander, H (1973) Tales of Yoruba Gods and Heroes. Greenwich, CT: Fawcett.

Cruz, RR (1995) Carrego de Egum: Contribuição aos Estudos do Rito Mortuário no Candomblé. PhD dissertation, Universidade Federal do Rio de Janeiro.

Cruz, RR (2003) O saber medicinal dos terreiros. In Silva, JM (ed.), Religiões Afro-Brasileiras e Saúde. São Luís: ProjetoAtó-Ire–Centro de Cultura Negra do Maranhão.

Cruz, RR (2018) Orô e Axé – a lógica e a função do sacrifício animal no Candomblé. YouTube. https://youtu.be/IoJ2kWaoDYg.

Csordas, TJ (1990) Embodiment as a paradigm for anthropology. Ethos 18, 5–47.

Cunha, MC (1980) Arte afro-brasileira. In Zanini, W (ed.), História Geral da Arte no Brasil. São Paulo: Instituto Moreira Sales.

Cunha, MO (1986) Em busca de um espaço: a linguagem gestual no Candomblé de Angola. PhD dissertation, Universidade de São Paulo.

Daniel, Y (2005) Dancing Wisdom: Embodied Knowledge in Haitian Vodou, Cuban Yoruba, and Bahian Candomblé. Chicago: University of Illinois Press.

De Cruz, H (2018) Etiological challenges to religious practices. American Philosophical Quarterly 55, 329–340.

Elbein dos Santos, J (1976/2012) Os Nàgô e a morte: pàde, àsèsè e o culto ègun na Bahia. Petrópolis: Vozes.

Engler, S (2019) Book Review / Comptes rendu: The Fetish Revisited: Marx, Freud, and the Gods Black People Make. Studies in Religion/Sciences Religieuses 48(2), 306–309.

Engler, S and Brito, E (2016) Afro-Brazilian and indigenous-influenced religions. In Schmidt, BE and Engler, S (eds.), Handbook of Contemporary Religions in Brazil. Leiden: Brill, pp. 142–169.

Engler, S and Isaia, AC (2016) Kardecism. In Schmidt, BE and Engler, S (eds.), Handbook of Contemporary Religions in Brazil. Leiden: Brill, pp. 186–203.

Fayemi, AK (2012) Philosophical problem of evil: Response to E. O. Oduwole. Philosophia: International Journal of Philosophy 4, 1–15.

Flaksman, C (2016) Relações e narrativas: o enredo no Candomblé da Bahia. Religião e Sociedade, 36, 13–33.

Flood, G (2013) Sacrifice as refusal. In Zachhuber, J and Meszaros, J (eds.), Sacrifice and Modern Thought. Oxford: Oxford University Press, pp. 115–131.

Fuller, CJ (2004) The Camphor Flame: Popular Hinduism and Society in India. Princeton, NJ: Princeton University Press.

Gama, LB (2009) Kosi Ejé Kosi Orixá: Simbolismo e Representações do Sangue no Candomblé. PhD dissertation, Universidade Federal de Pernambuco.

Gbadegesin, S (2013) African religions. In Taliaferro, C, Harrison, VS and Goetz, S (eds.), The Routledge Companion to Theism. London: Routledge, pp. 102–113.

Geertz, C (1973) The Interpretation of Cultures: Selected Essays. New York: Basic Books.

Gell, A (1998) Art and Agency: An Anthropological Theory. Oxford: Clarendon Press.

Gibson, JJ (1979) The Ecological Approach to Visual Perception. Boston, MA: Houghton Mifflin.

Goldman, M (2007) How to learn in an Afro-Brazilian spirit possession religion: Ontology and multiplicity in Candomblé. In Berliner, D and Sarró, R (eds.), Learning Religion: Anthropological Approaches. New York: Berghahn Books, pp. 103–119.

Goldman, M (2009) An Afro-Brazilian theory of the creative process: An essay in anthropological symmetrization. Social Analysis 53(2), 108–129.

Goldman, M (2012) O dom e a iniciação revisitados: o dado e o feito em religiões de matriz africana no Brasil. Mana 8(2), 269–288.

Gomberg, E (2011) Hospital de Orixás: Encontros terapêuticos em um terreiro de Candomblé. Salvador: Edufba.

Griffiths, P and Scarantino, A (2008) Emotions in the wild: The situated perspective on emotions. In Robbins, P and Aydede, M (eds.) The Cambridge Handbook of Situated Cognition. Cambridge: Cambridge University Press, 437–453.

Hallowell, AI (1960) Ojibwa ontology, behavior, and world view. In Diamond, S (ed.), Culture in History. New York: Columbia University Press, pp. 19–52.

Halloy, A (2012) Gods in the Flesh: Learning Emotions in the Xangô Possession Cult (Brazil). Ethnos 77 (2), 177–202.

Halloy, A (2013) Objects, bodies and gods: A cognitive ethnography of an ontological dynamic in the Xangô cult (Recife, Brazil). In Espirito Santo, D & Tassi, N (eds.), Making Spirits: Materiality and Transcendence in Contemporary Religions. London: Bloomsbury, pp. 133–158.

Halloy, A (2021) Transe de possession et affordances affectives. Ethnographie d'un mode d'interaction inter- et intra-personnelles. In Chauvaud, S, Defiolle, R and Valetopoulos, F (eds.), La palette des émotions. Comprendre les émotions en sciences sociales. Rennes: Presses Universitaires de Rennes, pp. 207–231.

Harding, RE (2006) É a Senzala: Slavery, women, and embodied knowledge in Afro-Brazilian Candomblé. In Griffith, RM and Savage, BD (eds.), Women and Religion in the African Diaspora: Knowledge, Power, and Performance. Baltimore, MD: Johns Hopkins University Press, pp. 3–18.

Hedley, D (2011) Sacrifice Imagined: Violence, Atonement, and the Sacred. London: Bloomsbury.

Hick, J (2004) An Interpretation of Religion: Human Responses to the Transcendent, 2nd ed. Basingstoke: Palgrave Macmillan.

Hickson, M (2013) A brief history of problems of evil. In McBrayer, JP and Howard-Snyder, D (eds.), The Blackwell Companion to the Problem of Evil. Oxford: Wiley-Blackwell, pp. 3–18.

Hubert, H and Mauss, M (1899) Essai sur la nature et la function du sacrifice. L'Année sociologique 2, 29–138.

Hufendiek, R (2016) Affordances and the normativity of emotions. Synthese 194 (11), 4455–4476.

Idowu, EB (1962) Olódùmarè: God in Yoruba Belief. London: Longmans.

Ingold, T (2001). From the transmission of representations to the education of attention. In Whitehouse, H (ed.), The Debated Mind: Evolutionary Psychology versus Ethnography. London: Routledge, pp. 114–153.

Johnson, PC (2002) Secrets, Gossip, and Gods: The Transformation of Brazilian Candomblé. Oxford: Oxford University Press.

Kato, BH (1975) Theological Pitfalls in Africa. Kisumu: Evangel.

Knepper, TD (2013) The Ends of Philosophy of Religion: Terminus and Telos. New York: Palgrave Macmillan.

Krueger, J and Colombetti, G (2018) Affective affordances and psychopathology. Discipline Filosofiche 2(18), 221–247.

Latour, B (1987) Science in Action. Cambridge, MA: Harvard University Press.

Latour, B (1996/2010) On the Modern Cult of the Factish Gods. Durham, NC: Duke University Press.

Léo Neto, N, Brooks, SE and Alves, RRN (2009) From Eshu to Obatala: Animals used in sacrificial rituals at Candomblé 'terreiros' in Brazil. Journal of Ethnobiology and Ethnomedicine 5, 1–10.

Liénard, P (2003) Le comportement rituel: Communication, cognition et action. PhD dissertation, Université Libre de Bruxelles.

Liénard, P (2006) The making of peculiar artifacts: Living kind, artifact and social order in the Turkana sacrifice. Journal of Cognition and Culture 6(3–4), 343–373.

Lima, VC (1977) A família-de-santo nos candomblés Jeje-Nagôs da Bahia: Um estudo de relações intra-grupais. Master's dissertation, Universidade Federal da Bahia.

Marques, L (2018) Fazendo orixás: sobre o modo de existência das coisas no Candomblé Religião e Sociedade 38(2), 221–243.

Marques, L (2022) Learning to learn in Candomblé: Notes on paths, knowledge, and the "education of distraction." Religion 52(1), 122–137.

Marques, L (2023) On the art of forging gods: Techniques, forces and materials in an Afro-Brazilian religion. In Jallo, Z (ed.), Material Culture in Transit. London: Routledge, pp. 185–200.

Matory, JL (2018) The Fetish Revisited: Marx, Freud, and the Gods Black People Make. Durham, NC: Duke University Press.

Mbiti, J (1970) Concepts of God in Africa. London: SPCK.

Merleau-Ponty, M (1945) Phénoménologie de la perception. Paris: Gallimard.

Miller, D (2005) Materiality: An introduction. In Miller, D (ed.), Materiality. Durham, NC: Duke University Press, pp. 1–52.

Motta, R (1991) Edje Bale: Alguns Aspectos do Sacrifício no Xangô Pernambucano. Recife: Universidade Federal de Pernambuco.

Motta, R (2005) Body trance and word trance in Brazilian religion. Current Sociology 53(2), 293–308.

Nagasawa, Y (2008) A new defence of Anselmian theism. The Philosophical Quarterly 58, 577–596.

Nina Rodrigues, R (1935) O Animismo Fetichista dos Negros Baianos. Rio de Janeiro: Civilização Brasileira.

Oduwole, EO (2007) The dialectics of ire (goodness) and ibi (evilness): An African understanding of the philosophical problem of evil. Philosophia: International Journal of Philosophy 31, 1–13.

Ogunnaike, A (2020) What's really behind the mask: A reexamination of syncretism in Brazilian Candomblé. Journal of Africana Religions 8, 146–171.

Oladipo, O (2004) Religion in African Culture: Some Conceptual Issues. In Wiredu K (ed.), A Companion to African Philosophy. Malden, MA: Blackwell, pp. 355–363.

Oliveira, AB (2009) Elégùn: A Iniciação no Candomblé, 3rd ed. Rio de Janeiro: Pallas.

p'Bitek, O (1971) African Religions in Western Scholarship. Nairobi: Literature Bureau.

Paton, D (2009). Obeah acts: Producing and policing the boundaries of religion in the Caribbean. Small Axe 13(1), 1–18.

Pérez, E (2022) The Gut: A Black Atlantic Alimentary Tract. Cambridge: Cambridge University Press.

Phillips, DZ (2001) Religion and the Hermeneutics of Contemplation. Cambridge: Cambridge University Press.

Porcher, JE (2021) Abrindo caminhos em filosofia da religião pela incorporação de tradições afro-brasileiras. Revista Brasileira de Filosofia da Religião 8(2), 72–82.

Porcher, JE and Carlucci, F (2023) Afro-Brazilian religions and the prospects for a philosophy of religious practice. Religions 14(2), 146.

Porcher, JE (2024) The mythic narratives of Candomblé Nagô and what they imply about its Supreme Being. Religious Studies, 1–17.

Prandi, R (2001) Mitologia dos Orixás. São Paulo: Companhia das Letras.

Rabelo, MCM (2011) Estudar a religião a partir do corpo: algumas questões teórico-metodológicas. Caderno CRH 24(61), 15–28.

Rabelo, MCM (2015) Aprender a ver no candomblé. Horizontes Antropológicos 21 (44), 229–251.

Rabelo, MCM and Santos, RMB (2011) Notas sobre o aprendizado no candomblé. Revista da FAEEBA – Educação e Contemporaneidade 20(35), 187–200.

Ramstead, MJD, Veissière, SPL and Kirmayer, LJ (2016) Cultural affordances: Scaffolding local worlds through shared intentionality and regimes of attention. Frontiers in Psychology 7,1090.

Ray, BC (1976) African Religions: Symbol, Ritual, and Community. Englewood Cliffs, NJ: Prentice-Hall.

Rocha, AM (2000) Caminhos de Odu. Rio de Janeiro: Pallas.

Rorty, R (1991) Solidarity or objectivity? In Objectivity, Relativism, and Truth: Philosophical Papers, vol. 1. Cambridge: Cambridge University Press, pp. 21–34. www.cambridge.org/core/books/objectivity-relativism-and-truth/04DFAEAC5991EC3C403C50B83C6F4086.

Rowe, W (1979) The problem of evil and some varieties of atheism. American Philosophical Quarterly 16, 335–341.

Russell, B (1910–1911) Knowledge by acquaintance and knowledge by description. Proceedings of the Aristotelian Society, *n.s.* 11, 108–128.

Ryle, G (1945–1946) Knowing how and knowing that. Proceedings of the Aristotelian Society, *n.s.* 46, 1–16.

Ryle, G (2009) Collected Papers, Vol. 2: Collected Essays, 1929–1968. London: Routledge.

Sansi-Roca, R (2005) The hidden life of stones: Historicity, materiality and the value of Candomblé objects in Bahia. Journal of Material Culture 10(2), 139–156.

Sansi, R (2009) "Fazer o santo": dom, iniciação e historicidade nas religiões afro-brasileiras. Análise Social 44(1), 139–160.

Schilbrack, K (2002) Introduction: On the use of philosophy in the study of myths. In Schilbrack, K (ed.), Thinking Through Myths: Philosophical Perspectives. London: Routledge, pp. 1–17.

Schilbrack, K (2014) Philosophy and the Study of Religions: A Manifesto. Malden, MA: Wiley-Blackwell.

Schilbrack K (2021) Religious practices and the formation of subjects. In Eckel, MD, Speight, CA and DuJardin, T (eds.), The Future of the Philosophy of Religion. Cham: Springer, pp. 43–60.

Schilbrack, K (2023) The danger in diversifying philosophy of religion. In Loewen, NRB and Rostalska, A (eds.), Diversifying Philosophy of Religion: Critiques, Methods, and Case Studies. London: Bloomsbury, 297–311.

Schmidt, BE (2013) Animal sacrifice as symbol of the paradigmatic other in the 21st century: Ebó, the offerings to African Gods, in the Americas. In Zachhuber, J and Meszaros, J (eds.), Sacrifice and Modern Thought. Oxford: Oxford University Press, pp. 197–213.

Schmidt, BE (2016) Spirits and Trance in Brazil: An Anthropology of Religious Experience. London: Bloomsbury.

Schmidt, BE (2024) Axé as the cornerstone of Candomblé philosophy and its significance for an understanding of well-being (bem estar). Religious Studies, 1–13.

Schmidt, BE and Engler, S (2016) Handbook of Contemporary Religions in Brazil. Leiden: Brill.

Segato, RL (2005) Santos e Daimones, 2nd ed. Brasília: Editora UnB.

Seligman, R (2014) Possessing Spirits and Healing Selves: Embodiment and Transformation in an Afro-Brazilian Religion. London: Palgrave Macmillan.

Sikka, S (2023) Is philosophy of religion racist? In Loewen, NRB and Rostalska, A (eds.), Diversifying Philosophy of Religion: Critiques, Methods, and Case Studies. London: Bloomsbury, 81–93.

Silva, VG and Brumana, FG (2016) Candomblé: Religion, world vision and experience. In Schmidt, BE and Engler, S (eds.), Handbook of Contemporary Religions in Brazil. Leiden: Brill, pp. 170–185.

Silveira, APL (2008) Batuque de Mulheres: Aprontando Tamboreiras de Nação nas Terreiras de Pelotas e Rio Grande, RS. Master's dissertation, Universidade Federal do Rio Grande do Sul.

Smart, N (1996) Dimensions of the Sacred: An Anatomy of the World's Beliefs. Berkeley: University of California Press.

Stewart, J (2008) Cosmopolitan communication ethics understanding and action: Religion and dialogue. In Roberts, KG and Arnett, RC (eds.), Communication Ethics: Between Cosmopolitanism and Provinciality. New York: Peter Lang, pp. 105–119.

Swinburne, R (2004) The Existence of God, 2nd ed. Oxford: Oxford University Press.

Tomasello, M (1999) The Cultural Origins of Human Cognition. Cambridge, MA: Harvard University Press.

Tomasello, M (2006) Why Don't Apes Point? In Enfield, NJ and Levinson, SC (eds.), Roots of Human Sociality: Culture, Cognition, and Interaction. Oxford: Berg, pp. 506–524.

Van Eyghen, H (2023) The Epistemology of Spirit Beliefs. London: Routledge.

Verger, PF (1985/2019) Lendas Africanas dos Orixás. Salvador: Fundação Pierre Verger.

Viveiros de Castro, E (2011) Zeno and the art of anthropology: Of lies, beliefs, paradoxes, and other truths. Common Knowledge 17(1), 128–145.

Vogel, A, Mello, MAS and Barros, JFP (1993) A Galinha-d'Angola: Iniciação e Identidade na Cultura Afro-Brasileira. Niterói: EDUFF.

Wafer, J (1991) The Taste of Blood: Spirit Possession in Brazilian Candomblé. Philadelphia: University of Pennsylvania Press.

Wiredu, K (1998) Toward decolonizing African philosophy and religion. African Studies Quarterly 1, 17–46.

Zagzebski, L (2011) Epistemic self-trust and the consensus gentium argument. In Clark, KJ and VanArragon, RJ (eds.), Evidence and Religious Belief. Oxford: Oxford University Press, pp. 22–36.

# Acknowledgments

Like Exu, the one who opens pathways, the John Templeton Foundation and the Brazilian Association for the Philosophy of Religion must be acknowledged first for their respective funding and management of the grant associated with the project "Expanding the Philosophy of Religion by Engaging with Afro-Brazilian Traditions" (grant #62101).

Throughout the project, I was warmly welcomed by the Leeds Centre for Philosophy of Religion and Theology, the Rutgers Center for the Philosophy of Religion, and the Birmingham Centre for Philosophy of Religion. Their support was crucial to the progress and success of this endeavor.

Gratitude extends to all who provided opportunities for me to articulate my thoughts. Thanks are due to the audiences at the University of Leeds, the University of Birmingham, Waseda University, the Logic & Religion Webinar, the Jesuit School of Philosophy and Theology, the University of Brasília, and the Federal Universities of Juiz de Fora, Bahia, Rio de Janeiro, and Rio Grande do Sul. Special appreciation goes to the students of two modules I taught at the Federal University of Santa Maria for their patience and engagement.

Enriching conversations and valuable feedback were provided by Mikel Burley, Daniel De Luca–Noronha, Steven Engler, Agnaldo Portugal, Bettina Schmidt, Kevin Schilbrack, Tasia Scrutton, and Marciano Spica. I also appreciate the assistance of Marcus Welby and André Bonfim, who facilitated my access to *terreiros* in Bahia, and to Wagner Ludwig Malta, Lucas Marques, and Bettina Schmidt for allowing me to reproduce their photographs.

Appreciation also goes to the series editor, Yujin Nagasawa, for the inspiration and platforms provided by the Global Philosophy of Religion Project, and for his generous hospitality during my time in Birmingham.

Lastly, I extend my sincere gratitude to Pedro Pricladnitzky and Magda Togni for their friendship over the last twenty years, and to Fernanda Fedrizzi for her love and unwavering support. This work is humbly dedicated to her.

# Cambridge Elements ☰

# Global Philosophy of Religion

## Yujin Nagasawa
*University of Oklahoma*

Yujin Nagasawa is Kingfisher College Chair of the Philosophy of Religion and Ethics and Professor of Philosophy at the University of Oklahoma. He is the author of *The Problem of Evil for Atheists* (2024), *Maximal God: A New Defence of Perfect Being Theism* (2018), *Miracles: A Very Short Introduction* (2018), *The Existence of God: A Philosophical Introduction* (2011), and *God and Phenomenal Consciousness* (2008), along with numerous articles. He is the editor-in-chief of *Religious Studies* and served as the president of the British Society for the Philosophy of Religion from 2017 to 2019.

## About the Series

This Cambridge Elements series provides concise and structured overviews of a wide range of religious beliefs and practices, with an emphasis on global, multi-faith viewpoints. Leading scholars from diverse cultural backgrounds and geographical regions explore topics and issues that have been overlooked by Western philosophy of religion.

## Cambridge Elements ☰

# Global Philosophy of Religion

### Elements in the Series

*Afro-Brazilian Religions*
José Eduardo Porcher

A full series listing is available at: www.cambridge.org/EGPR

Printed in the United States
by Baker & Taylor Publisher Services